Going to Extremes

For Linne Matthews, my editor, who did a great job working on my own most enjoyable writing project.

Going to Extremes

*The Adventurous Life of
Harry de Windt*

Stephen Wade

PEN & SWORD
DISCOVERY

First published in Great Britain in 2016 by
PEN AND SWORD DISCOVERY
an imprint of
Pen and Sword Books Ltd
47 Church Street
Barnsley
South Yorkshire S70 2AS

ISBN 978 147386 354 5

Printed and bound in England
by CPI Group (UK) Ltd, Croydon, CR0 4YY

Typeset in Times New Roman by
CHIC GRAPHICS

Pen & Sword Books Ltd incorporates the imprints of Pen & Sword
Archaeology, Atlas, Aviation, Battleground, Discovery,
Family History, History, Maritime, Military, Naval, Politics, Railways,
Select, Social History, Transport, True Crime, Claymore Press,
Frontline Books, Leo Cooper, Praetorian Press, Remember When,
Seaforth Publishing and Wharncliffe.

For a complete list of Pen and Sword titles please contact
Pen and Sword Books Limited
47 Church Street, Barnsley, South Yorkshire, S70 2AS, England
E-mail: enquiries@pen-and-sword.co.uk
Website: www.pen-and-sword.co.uk

Contents

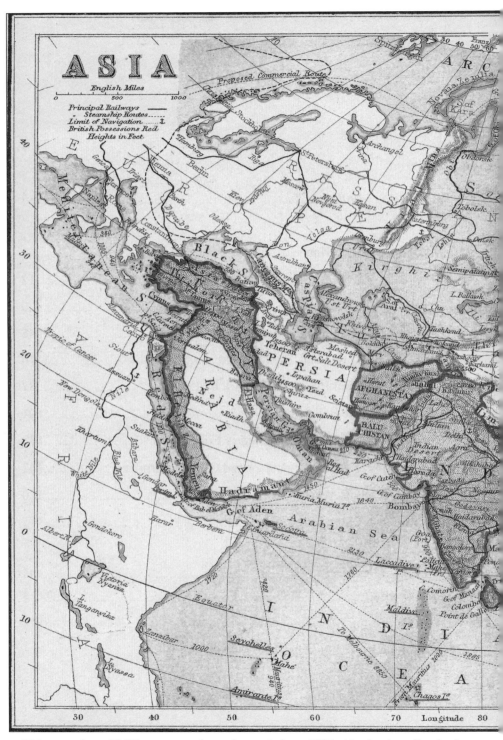

This map from Phillips geographers shows Asia c. 1900. (Author's collection)

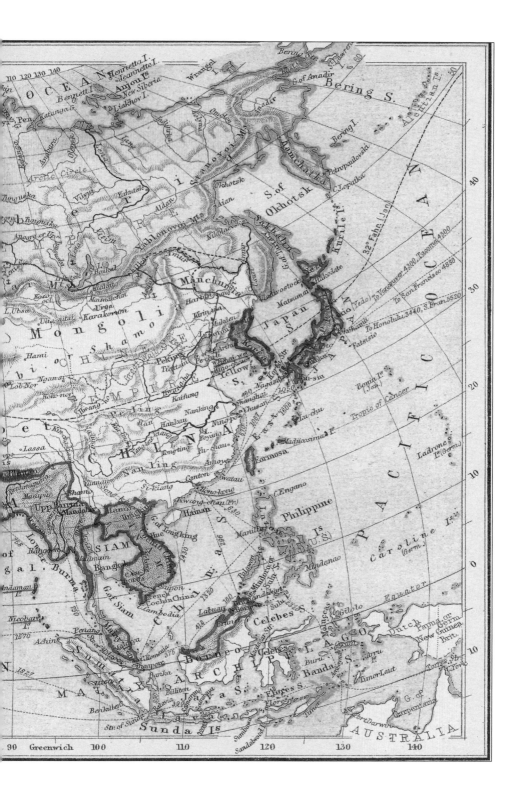

Chapter 1

Meet Harry

What was the object of this stupendous voyage? ... another reason is one with which I fancy most Englishmen will readily sympathize ... the feat had never before been performed.

Harry de Windt on his book
From Paris to New York by Land

On 12 February 1908, a line of cars were revving up on Broadway, New York, ready for an epic journey to Paris. They were to drive first down to San Francisco, then be shipped to Alaska, and then over the Bering Straits to Siberia. From there the route was overland for thousands of miles to Europe, and finally to Paris. A quarter of a million people lined the New York streets to cheer them. It was to be an arduous, gruelling trek, and the winner was a Protos, driven by Lieutenant Hans Koeppen, who entered Paris on 26 July. The whole affair was a huge celebration of technological prowess, and, of course, human endurance. The media loved it. In a sense, this could not have happened had it not been for one man's seemingly crazed vision of a journey across this vast distance, twenty years earlier. His name was Harry de Windt.

Harry was an obsessive traveller, and getting close to him starts with a simple question: why do people travel? Why, in particular, did so many Victorians travel – often to distant and dangerous areas of the globe? The answers were provided by the Vicar of Harrow, as quoted in a work on European travel. He wrote that the great bulk of travellers in his time (c.1850) were motivated by 'restlessness, by an ill-defined curiosity, by ennui, by the love of dissipation, by a spirit of wandering, by a fancied regard to works of art, by the love of novelty ... by the

1

superabundance of money'. This book is the story of a man who travelled for all these reasons except the fourth, as he always looked down disapprovingly on 'dissipation'. He is Harry de Windt, the Bear Grylls of the 1890s, all-round good sport, and in fact the sort of man you would want on your side if you were in a tight corner.

He was a short, wiry man, accustomed to leading rather than following; he could handle a pistol as well as a horsewhip; he could act the playboy in a casino, the jockey in a professional handicap plate, or endure a blizzard in some God-forsaken back of beyond. He remained a gentleman in all situations and expected other men to have the same moral compass. He believed, confirming George Bernard Shaw's definition of a gentleman, that he should put more into life than he took out of it. Nevertheless, in between the tough expeditions, he loved his creature comforts.

In an age of literary adventurers and global travellers, he stands out as a Renaissance man. Across the span of his impressive number of books produced both while moving around the world and in between, when he recovered from the privations of his foolhardy treks across barren lands, the reader catches glimpses of this man of tireless energy. One time he is lying in a posting station hut in Siberia, battling frostbite; then he may be seen riding a chaser over fences on an English racecourse; and then perhaps there may be a sight of him lecturing from the platform in America, or having dinner with Teddy Roosevelt. These, when assembled, form a profile of the man known to his contemporaries mainly as the explorer, the wiry little man who had stories of travel spinning from him like a web of constant entertainment. He is at once both a typical Victorian and Edwardian clubman and a whimsical, humorous dilettante, dipping into the occult, palmistry and fringe medicine. There is a Harry de Windt for the reader who loves travel narratives of extreme courage and endurance; a Harry de Windt for the lover of the *bon viveur* who swapped tales with Oscar Wilde, Arthur Conan Doyle and a host of other celebrities; and a Harry de Windt who could be the man of action, the commandant of a prisoner of war camp in the Great War – a man whom one of his charges described as 'a thin little man who was the very Devil'.

2

Then there is my own Harry: the man who is a gift and a delight for any biographer.

Biography begins with some kind of empathic link between writer and subject, and there is always a first impression that invites the writer to tell the life in focus. Simply, the reason for this, in Harry's case, is the sheer delight of his company. His books – particularly his reminiscences – are collections of compulsive anecdotes, ranging from momentous meetings with fascinating people to confrontations that bring death perilously close. To settle down in a comfortable chair with any of his books is to accompany a rich, fertile imagination on a long, constantly diverting journey, whether that be by train from Paris to Moscow, or standing with him in sheer boredom waiting for a ticket to cross the Channel as the Great War breaks out all around him.

His portrait in the one book he wrote about his life, in 1913, shows him in evening dress: a full moustache, a stiff, starched high collar, hair immaculately oiled flat, and a bow tie neatly complementing his smart jacket. This is Harry de Windt, known at the time as a traveller. He was a man full of stories. The summaries of his chapters tell it all: 'My first expedition; a French Don Juan' and 'An interesting blackguard; I meet Madame de Novikoff'. A glance at his style reveals the archetypal club raconteur. Here was a man who could entertain, who could project himself to an audience. He was a man who had lived, seen the world, mixed with all classes and all nations. Any London gathering of intellectuals, movers and shakers of the world would have wanted him sat at their tables.

He was a member of several clubs, and his account of one of them perhaps represents the typical nature of these places: 'Another club to which I then belonged was the old Pelican in Denman Street … it was essentially a sporting and bohemian club and its supporters were of all grades of society, from the most distinguished members of the peerage to the lesser lights of the stage.' He goes on to mention several of the more renowned members: 'Fred Leslie and Arthur Roberts, who were then drawing the town, the one at the Gaiety and the other at the Avenue [theatres], were nightly habitués of the club and were ready

3

to 'oblige', and were always accompanied by such artists at the piano as Teddy Solomon and Lionel Monckton.'

Harry had always been clubbable, but a look at his restless life will explain why he was such a valuable club member.

Ever since the Great Game, that epic mind game between Britain and Russia, had warmed up around the 1830s and then started boiling over after the Crimean War thirty years later, the Brits who had the urge to travel had been drawn to Russia and to India. It was something that seemed to counter the rather safer venture of the well-established Grand Tour of cultural Europe. Looking at statues and old paintings was a sound occupation for a gentleman, but now that the thin red line had proved itself against Napoleon and then the Russians on the borders of their own great empire, a gentleman felt the pull of the East.

By the 1890s, these plucky gentlemen, many of them army officers, had learned a number foreign tongues, investigated suitable outfits for deserts vast and mountains formidable, and with their men servants, they had met the challenge of what was still referred to at the time as a 'savage' part of the known world.

Harry now stands out as the adventurer *par excellence* of the 1890s and early 1900s. This is Harry Willes Darell de Windt, who was born in Paris in 1856, with aristocratic forebears and a sure sense of his abilities from early on. Harry was one of the first writers I discovered from this great age of adventure, when there were still headhunters, wolves and cannibals in some unspeakable regions of the earth. I bought a rather dog-eared copy of *From Paris to New York by Land*, saw a photo of the author dressed in the most engulfing, surreal anorak I had ever seen, and read on, transfixed by his stories.

Harry, I later learned, had crammed so much into his life that he must have been weighed down by the weight of dashing, hair-raising memories as he grew older. After all, he had been more than simply a traveller across steppes and prairies: here was a man who had been an expert on Russian Siberian prisons and a figure in the British turf, had formed a company to find gold in the Klondike, and been commandant of a prison camp in the Great War. Before all this he had sampled that mystic East, being *aide de camp* to his brother-in-law, the Rajah of

Sarawak. Harry was only twenty when he went east for the first time.

Of course, people have emotional, private lives too. In Harry's case, this was formed on three marriages, his last one being to the actress Elaine Inescourt (her real name being Charlotte Ihle). In the last phase of his life, from about 1920, he had at last settled down to be writer, speaker and matey companion to people in all walks of neo-Georgian life. He even turned up as a witness in a famous trial involving Lord Alfred Douglas.

Writing his life has always been steadily in progress, the material slowly gathering as I wrote other biographies. Now, in 2016, it appears that there is still no biographer to tell the world about this remarkable man, someone who represents the essential qualities of the Victorian writer-adventurer. He always had the urge to talk of his travels, and became a popular lecturer both in Britain and America; he was an inveterate letter writer to the press and loved a debate, relishing the controversy over the true nature of the conditions in Siberian prisons.

His writing emerged at the time of the great male adventure fiction – the world of Rider Haggard and Conan Doyle – but he was also there, at the centre of things, when the imperial wars still raged, and when Britain's militaristic culture had an insatiable appetite for, as Shakespeare's Othello put it, stories of places 'where men's heads do grow beneath their shoulders/ and where men do each other eat.'

He was also in some important places when great imaginative writers converged on these hot spots: he went to Sakhalin prison settlement close to the time when Anton Chekhov visited there; and he was in the Klondike when Jack London and Robert Service knew the gold fields. Closer to home, he was a clubman in an age of literary diners and societies of male enthusiasts for travel and for good causes.

Maybe, like so many men who had missed out on participating in the Great War, he needed a 'test' of some kind. After all, his grandfather was a naval hero, in both the Napoleonic Wars and in the later Opium Wars – Captain John Willes Johnson; and his mother was a daughter of the Vicomte de Rastignac, who had fought with Napoleon. That paradox in his roots – people *pro* and *con* the great

Emperor – has a certain dramatic interest, and above so much else, Harry loved a sense of drama, as his portraits show – a dapper, athletic man, aware of his self-image and eager to be what a proper gentleman should be: in control, suave, assured. The pictures we have show a man who could cope with a Siberian winter and face a wild band of rascals in the middle of nowhere. Yet, in complete contrast, he seems to be there or thereabouts in a long list of scandals, confrontations and oppositions. In researching the life of Lord Alfred Douglas, for instance, there was Harry, a member of the Lord Kitchener and Battle of Jutland Committee, in 1923, with General Cyril Prescott-Decie and Lady Edith Fox-Pitt; Douglas and the Committee gathered to expound the view that Churchill was partly responsible for Kitchener's death.

Harry, fresh from his first taste of the East, now saw that one of the world's most formidable challenges lay before him: a trek involving, in some way, the vastness of Siberia. The very name evoked then – and still does – horrendous penal settlements and, more recently, the Gulags. What was the Russian penal system like in the mid to late nineteenth century?

In his story *Punin and Baburin* (1874), Ivan Turgenev describes a scene in which a young man, Yumil, from a huge peasant-run estate, is sent to Siberia:

> The unfortunate boy was being transported to a settlement; on the other side of the fence was a little cart loaded with his poor belongings. Such were the times then. Yumil stood without his cap, with downcast head, barefoot, with his boots tied up with a string behind his back and his face turned up to the seigneurial mansion. … A stupid smile was frozen on his colourless lips …

In the penal system of the Russian Empire, known as *katorga*, Siberian work camps provided the ideal destination for the underclass, who could be used on public works to develop those regions that were several time zones away from Moscow. These camps were first established back in the seventeenth century; it was realized that no one could escape, as they were in one of the most inhospitable regions on earth. Supervision was therefore no real problem and if a few prisoners did take a chance against nature, then they were expendable. When the penal laws were overhauled in 1847 with the rise of nationalism, and a growing number of dissidents who had to be removed to the extremities of the empire, these exiles mixed with peasant and criminal classes. Other minorities were sent there also; notably the Poles, who were known as Sybiraks.

In the 1870s, there was a renewed interest by intellectuals and students from Moscow and St Petersburg in the peasant as an idealized type with special virtues. This movement made people generally more aware of the vulnerability of the peasants, as in Turgenev's account of the boy, Yumil. In other words, people could be sent to the camps by the Russian equivalent of manorial lords, as well as by judicial professionals. The Narodniks, the intellectuals who were fervent for the cause of the land workers, helped to make the nature of *katorga* more visible and understood. One of the most forthright accounts of the system comes from the writer Anton Chekhov, who went to Sakhalin island, known formally as Sakhalin Oblast, a remote island north of Japan over 400 miles long.

For a *katorga*, this was as far east as anyone could go in Russia. Chekhov went there in 1891 to investigate conditions, mainly in a medical role (he was a doctor), and the result was his book *The Island of Sakhalin*. In his letters home, he wrote about the long journey there, by carriage and river boat, and after the time there, he was savage and indignant on the whole *katorga* system. This passage from a letter to his friend Alexei Suvorin encapsulates his criticism:

> Sakhalin is a place of unbearable suffering, on a scale of which no creature but man is capable, whether he be free or in chains. People who have worked there or in that region have faced terrifying problems and responsibilities which they continue to work towards resolving. I am not a sentimental person, otherwise I should say that we should make pilgrimages to places like Sakhalin as the Turks go to Mecca, and sailors and

penal experts should study Sakhalin in the same way that soldiers study Sevastopol.

In terms of the political exiles, as opposed to the criminals, there were marked differences. What was called the 'Administrative Process' was applied, meaning a secret tribunal – a trial with no press reports. The English traveller Harry de Windt travelled to Siberia at the same time that Chekhov was on Sakhalin, and de Windt explains: 'A man may be seated quietly at home with his family, in his office … when the fatal touch on the shoulder summons him away, perhaps for ever. The sentence once passed, there is no appeal to a higher court.'

Exiles usually spent up to two years in a prison in the west before Siberian exile, and then they went on their very long journey. In a string of towns across the Russian Far East, exiles lived at various stages in their sentence. As de Windt noted, there were concessions: 'On arrival at Irkutsk, prison-dress is discarded, although he remains under lock and key and in close charge of the Cossack who is responsible for his safe delivery.' The most detailed picture we have of life in the *katorga* in the nineteenth century is from Dostoyevsky's *Memoirs from the House of the Dead*, in which we have the place from the viewpoint of a political exile. He was sometimes in irons, wore regulation clothes according to his category, and worked as the common criminals did. But there was clearly a split between the criminals as such and what Dostoyevsky calls the 'gentlemen prisoners'. As in every community, though, there were ever lower echelons in which prisoners resided, and in this case, it was the category of Polish prisoners. The 'gentlemen' were at first reviled and had to win respect: 'They watched our sufferings, which we tried not to show them, with delight. We were particularly severely cursed at work at first, because we were not as strong as they were.'

The camp projects were mainly road making and timber work, and the Amur Cart Road – an incredible achievement that involved constructing a road 2,000 kilometres long through a massive area of swamps and desolate taiga wasteland. It took eleven years to build, being completed in 1909, and it was on a scale almost as large as some of the later Gulag projects. The conditions of life and work in Siberia were extremely severe, as Harry de Windt describes: 'Let the reader imagine, if possible, the blank despair of existence under such conditions: day after day, year after year, nothing to do or look at of interest; tortured by heat and mosquitoes in summer, perished by cold and hunger in the dark, cruel winter.'

Siberia extends for 4,830,000 square miles – eighty-three times the size of England and Wales. Organizing penal colonies across that vast space and beyond meant having a system of area managers. There were magistrates and police officers, but the army was the real presence in terms of overseeing the exiles and prisoners. There were as many complaints from members of the administration as there were from writers and travellers who, like Chekhov, lamented the desperately hard conditions of life.

This background explains the very heart of Harry's achievements. He was to become recognized as an authority on this penal system.

This was the man who, in the first years of the new century, often sat in his club – or someone else's club – and held forth on this rich experience. His life shows exactly what was at the heart of the club: the interchange of stories from one's life. Those who fought for, administered and generally travelled the empire came home with enough tales to entertain friends at lengthy dinners for decades. Harry was one of those men.

He was a friend of Oscar Wilde, and in fact, Harry's sister, who was the Ranee of Sarawak, became a close friend of Lady Wilde, Oscar's mother, and so there were connections before Harry met Oscar at the Savoy, where – at a dinner, of course – he was faced with a response to his new book on Russian prisons:

> But I was almost startled when my new book was, for a brief while, under discussion, at the violence with which Wilde attacked the latter, and my defence of Russian prisons of which (as he afterwards smilingly admitted) he knew absolutely nothing, and cared less! 'Any Englishman,' he

declared, 'who defends such a barbarous system should himself be banished to Siberia!'

'But I am only half an Englishman!' I protested.

'Then half of you should be exiled,' replied Oscar sternly, but with a twinkle in his eye.

Harry's life, as the son of a military man who had died young, and with French aristocratic ancestry, had the cachet to succeed in society, but that was not enough: one needed charm, and he had that in abundance. In the Edwardian war years, he was to find himself a prison commandant for internees, and so the literary man and traveller who called in at his clubs became a rarity: the prison governor. That was an occupation generally considered to be too low on the social scale to be accepted in high society, of course. But Harry being Harry, he was, in effect, classless, being able to mix with Siberian tribes equally as well as with lords and ladies back home.

The Victorians travelled for many reasons, including restlessness, trials of personal endurance, and the more pragmatic reasons of complementing the mainstream channels of travel supplied by the military and missionary imperatives. But fundamentally, when gentlemen and gentlewomen travelled independently, the motive was a dangerous but exciting mixture of curiosity and foolhardiness.

The roots of many itineraries lay in the eighteenth century 'Grand Tour', which had been safely restricted to the European sites of interest regarding the classical heritage of the new, burgeoning Enlightenment. As time went on, horizons expanded, in terms of both geographical knowledge and of more established means of communication.

In the context of Harry's aims and objectives, as a man who welcomed a challenge, there was the added dimension of the Great Game, a strategic interplay of information gathering and espionage involving the bold military men in the officer class of the British Army, and the Russian forces who were tasked with maintaining military intelligence in the wild borderlands of northern India and the Russian Far East, extending to the coast at Vladivostok.

Men with Harry's disposition, drawn to perilous encounters with nature and with the so-called 'savage' races beyond the pale of what was then designated as 'civilization', always had the option of contributing to the ongoing Great Game, but in spite of his marginal military status (being attached to a yeomanry battalion), when it came to journeys across Asia and into the vast wastelands of Siberia, he was the epitome of the English gentleman traveller.

Of course, it was always his intention to write about his travels and to publish these. Strangely though, in many ways he played down the writer in him. His overall attitude to Harry de Windt, the writer and speaker, was largely indifferent in that he saw it as nothing of any high literary quality. He saw his books and articles as the product of a trade, a journalistic activity that provided the 'bread and butter' income. Yet here was a man who moved in the social circles where literary men were to be found (see chapter 7); he was a close friend to many prominent writers of his time, and an acquaintance of many more. The last decades of Victoria's reign and the Edwardian years were an age of the bookman, and Harry was firmly placed in that category.

Chapter 2

From Illustrious Ancestors
to Sarawak

*So it came to pass that I was left at the age of fourteen
practically alone in the world, for my only sister had
married the Rajah of Sarawak.*

Harry de Windt, *My Restless Life*

The de Windt story begins, for the present purpose, in the Dutch
Antilles, and stretches, through a French connection, to Wiltshire. Yet
in spite of all this, Harry was a Brit. However, he always looked back
in his writings to the Paris he knew in his formative years, as he was
born in Paris and he invariably praised the Paris of the 1870s and '80s
as being a beautiful, golden age of elegance and culture. There was
always a Frenchman in him, shown to good effect in his love of good
cuisine and *bon ton* fashion, appearance and manners. All the pictures
we have of him show a smart, dandyish gentleman, with an air of
insouciance and *savoir faire*. As to the Dutch, that was always distant,
but in his autobiography, *My Restless Life*, he creates an apocryphal
lineage linking himself to the painter Peter de Wint: 'The names were
originally spelt alike, and we have the same coat of arms – "Four heads
proper blowing four winds".' He quotes a biographer of the artist also,
to good effect, '"The device conveys an appropriate idea of their
hereditary instincts which led them to emigrate to various countries,"
and in my case, perhaps, this is not incorrect.'

Still, he was of Dutch extraction, with the de Windts of the island
of St Eustatius as the main link to the more ancient scion of his
genealogy.

On his maternal side, Harry's roots reach back to France, where the de Windts were married into the Chapt de Rastignac aristocracy. Elizabeth de Windt Chapt de Rastignac married Captain John Willes Johnson, who was born at Monkton Combe, Somerset, in 1793. He was the grandson of the Leicester architect John Johnson, who is perhaps best known for his designs for Berner Street, The Jockey Club and the Shire Hall at Chelmsford.

Captain John Samuel Willes Johnson married Elisabeth de Windt in Paris on 14 May 1821.

Elisabeth was the heiress of Viscomtesse Judith de Windt, the widow of Jacques Gabriel, Viscount de Rastignac, who had a distinguished military career. Pierre Chapt de Rastignac (1769–1833) was a man of considerable power and importance in France. At the time of the Revolution, he was a Captain of Dragoons, and later, in 1791, he emigrated to the Caribbean.

Elisabeth's groom, of the Royal Navy, was also to be distinguished in action; he had entered the navy in 1807, and rose to the rank of captain by November, 1841, and at that point he commanded HMS *Wolverine*. One of his most celebrated moments was in 1809 when he was master's mate in a vessel that had material of great importance for military intelligence, as his citation for the Naval General Service Medal notes: 'he succeeded by a bold *ruse de guerre* in saving his charge from capture.' On another occasion, on the *Pallas*, he was highly commended for his part in 'a most bloody boat action in which casualties to both sides were terrible'. He also took part in a battle at La Sturia. The captain, whose full name was John Samuel Willes Johnson (his third name, Willes, being given to Harry), was also an author, and some of his DNA was perhaps behind Harry's temperament, as he published *The Traveller's Guide through France, Italy, Spain and Switzerland* in 1828.

Elisabeth died in April 1842. Her daughter, Elisabeth, married Captain Joseph Clayton Jennyns in 1851 at Épinay-sur-Orge, Seine, in August 1847. In 1851, Queen Victoria granted the Clayton-Jennyns by royal licence and authority the right to assume and use the surname de Windt. The reason given related to her uncle, who was Adolphus de Windt, and it was his high esteem that had made the adoption possible; he was the brother of Judith de Windt, the viscomtesse. In addition to this, Harry's father, Joseph Clayton, had such a distinguished record that of course his status would have helped to have the request granted. Joseph Clayton had served as a captain with the British Auxiliary Legion in Spain, and he had also received the Cross of San Fernando and a medal for his part in the capture of Irún in 1836, in the First Carlist Wars. The Cross of San Fernando is Spain's highest honour for gallantry, and it makes it clear that Joseph was fighting as a mercenary on the royalist side. He was with De Lacy Evans, who led the British Auxiliary Force, and at the Battle of Irún, in the Basque Country, he was involved in preserving the place for the royalist cause.

The wording of the award from Queen Victoria is as follows:

They may henceforth take the name of De Windt, in lieu of that of Jennyns, and that the said Joseph Clayton-Jennyns, may bear the arms of De Windt quarterly, in the first quarter, with those of Jennyns, and that of the said surname and arms may in like manner be taken, borne and used by their issue; such arms being first duly exemplified according to the laws of arms.

Why did the family adopt the name of de Windt? It appears to be a question of cachet, with the added dimension of a royal reward for Clayton Jennyns' service in the name of the monarchy in Spain when he was serving with de Lacy Evans. Harry's father was something of a firebrand and adventurer. The de Windt writings are peppered with accounts of duels, and when Harry was young his father's appearance provoked a duel: 'He was one day walking in Regent Street when a passer-by somewhat rudely drew his attention to the strange-looking neck-tie. My father instantly demanded an apology.' A duel was fought, with pistols, and as Harry recalls, 'a meeting took place … on the French coast, when my father escaping scathless, winged his man, for he was a good shot and had previously been out on two occasions.'

There is no way of avoiding the judgement that Clayton Jennyns de Windt, Harry's father, was an adventurer, a swashbuckler in the grand tradition of the soldier of fortune who goes out in search of danger and camaraderie. One result of his fighting alongside de Lacy Evans was that he was seen by all the right people as a sound royalist, a man for the protection of the landed establishment, and one who would extend that action into the Continent as well as at home. That image attached to his father would resonate down the years, as something that Harry would always find would figure when he was appraised by those in power.

Reading between the lines of Harry's own autobiographical writings, it becomes clear that although he takes it for granted that all the peers and fellows he meets and drinks with respect and accept him, his readers will understand why. Yet matters are not as simple as that from our viewpoint in the twenty-first century. The point is that the university men and the actors, writers and editors would find that their world often crossed into that of the sportsmen and politicians. The networks functioned wonderfully well, with the Masonic society and the aristocratic echelons working into the larger networks. Thus, when Harry planned a journey, he would know people who would write him a letter for the ambassador or the military attaché in some distant place on the planned route. Harry may not have been a renowned scholar at Magdalene College, but he could ride, drink, speechify, fire a gun and join a hunting party when required. He was the man you would ask to any gathering without fear of any *faux pas* or breech of good manners.

Elisabeth, Harry's grandmother, before being adopted as heiress by the Chapt de Rastignac, spent her early life in St Croix, in the West Indies. One outstanding feature of the island of St Eustatius was that it was neutral when wars raged around it, involving Britain, France and the United States; it was also noted as a very wealthy trading centre, notably for arms and munitions. It seems highly likely that Jan de Windt and Adolphus Roosevelt made connections with the Chapt de Rastignac, and somewhere in that social network there was a reason why young Elisabeth was taken into the Rastignac family, and settled at Épinay. Harry is silent on all this family history. Although there is no evidence here, clearly one suspects that there may have been a liaison, and that the Comte found himself the father of a little girl. Such situations were far from rare in that cultural context.

Harry had a lot to say about Épinay though. In his account of his birthplace he has fond and clear memories:

> We lived a few miles out of Paris, at the Chateau of Épinay-sur-Orge, where the solitary village street still bears our name, in white letters on a blue enamel plaque. … My mother … married an Englishman, Clayton Jennyns of the 15th Hussars, who assumed the name of de Windt and who, after his marriage, wore straight-brimmed hats and huge *noeuds-flottants* [bandanas], and otherwise adopted the manners and customs of France.

When de Rastignac returned from the West Indies, he obviously settled his second family at his chateau there; we know that from 1811 to 1817 he had that chateau built. After the demise of Napoleon, when the Bourbon dynasty resumed power, he became President of the Electoral College for the department of Charente. He had several other high positions, and just before his death, when the government of Louis Philippe was in power (in 1830) he had graduated to a lofty position in the First Chamber of the government. He died at the chateau in Épinay in October 1833.

As a young man, Harry became a Parisian; but he also knew the city of Boulogne, where the family rented a house in the Rue des Pipots. His memories of this time are overshadowed by the advent of cholera, and he described this in *My Restless Life*: 'At last the dread disease became so bad that we all left for Dieppe. … Here we stayed at the principal hotel, only to discover on the morning after our arrival that a guest had died on the previous night of the malady in rooms adjoining ours.'

There were three children: Harry, Margaret and George. George was born in 1848, Margaret in 1849, and Harry in 1856. There was to be a profound tragedy for them all, as their mother died in 1870, just before the outbreak of the Franco-Prussian War. As Harry noted, 'She therefore never witnessed the downfall of France, nor the occupation of our beloved chateau by Prussian Uhlans [lancers] … but when this occurred, Épinay was no longer ours.'

Harry's deep affection for his native France stayed with him all his life, and his references to Épinay are always fond and rather nostalgic. Paris was held equally in his affections – and he is rhapsodic on the beauty of that city in the 1870s in particular.

He came to know various parts of Northern France very well, including Boulogne, which was at the time notorious as the place to which wealthy Englishmen took their mistresses for arguably the sweetest experiences of their illicit liaisons. It was also a place where British debtors took refuge, so all in all, it was a place of great interest to a young man such as Harry. He writes of the city as a home for 'county court exiles' and quotes an old jibe:

Beautiful Boulogne! We laud thee in song,
The home of the stranger who's done something wrong!

Harry's father died in 1863, and *The Times* gave the essential facts in one succinct paragraph:

FATAL ACCIDENT: Captain Clayton Jennyns de Windt, of Blunsdon Hall, near Highworth, has been killed through a fall from his horse. He was proceeding to visit the widow of his late father-in-law, Captain Willes Johnson, who died on the 29th of last week. The horse took fright, and Captain de Windt was thrown into a ditch. He only breathed slightly when found, and died soon after. His wife and family were in France at the time of the occurrence.

There is a sadness in Harry's account of his being left as an orphan and under the power of the Court of Chancery, as he wrote in *My Restless Life* that he was, at fourteen, practically alone in the world after his sister Margaret married Sir Charles Brooke, Rajah of Sarawak, to become the Ranee (in effect, a queen). As for big brother

George, he died when he was just twenty-seven, in 1876. As a teenager, then, in the early 1870s, Harry was under the guidance of a tutor, tucked away in the country in Wiltshire. Harry, though a man of wide culture and many languages, was never an academic, and book learning was not something that attracted him. He had a miserable time with his tutor, as he later described:

> It was decided for some obscure reason to entrust me to the care of a West Country parson – an admirable man in his way, and one for whom I still retain a most affectionate memory. But I was his only pupil, and I still shudder at the recollection of the dreary days passed in that remote parish, where the only amusements consisted of an occasional Penny Reading or a gloomy croquet party! Moreover, I had no companions of my own age, for although my tutor was married, his olive-branches were still in the nursery.

With a long line of military types in the family, it is no surprise to learn that Harry fancied a life in the army; he also toyed with entering the Merchant Marine, until he learned about the hardships and torments involved in the life of a midshipman. His destiny was to be called to Sarawak, where his sister had played her part in having her little brother employed as *aide de camp* to the Rajah. Harry describes the momentous scene that provides his first foreign adventure – one that was to be followed by many more:

> The vicar saw me off at Southampton, which rather marred the pleasure of this golden hour of emancipation, for we had always been good friends, indeed almost comrades, and our parting recalled many acts of kindness which had, I fear, been but poorly repaid by my ungrateful self! And perhaps that is why, although it was a fine clear day, that familiar bowed and sombre figure appeared rather blurred and indistinct as the *Alpha* steamed out of harbour, and my old friend waved me a kindly farewell.

Thus I was launched, at the age of sixteen, on the hazardous highway of life.

In her memoirs of life in Sarawak, Margaret wrote only one paragraph about her brother, but it contains an important reflection on Harry's future. She writes about his work there as *aide de camp*, and notes:

This was a great joy to me, my brother and I being devoted to one another. I like to imagine that the interest he took in Sarawak and in the many expeditions on which he accompanied the Rajah, first inspired the travelling passion in him and led to his future achievements in the many world-wide expeditions … it was during his stay in Sarawak that he wrote his first book.

Sarawak is neatly defined in an atlas of 1890: 'A large territory to the west of Brunei, with a seaboard of about 400 miles and an area of 42,000 square miles, but the population scarcely numbers 500,000.' It has had self-government since 1963, from which date it became part of the Federation of Malaya. But in the early 1860s, being placed in the circle of islands that form the southern rim of the China Sea, it formed a very important location for British interests: very much a unique outpost, independent, with its own ruler, the Rajah. In terms of Harry's life, this was Charles Brooke, the Rajah in whose service he was to begin his wandering career; his employer was his brother-in-law.

To the west of the island, in the centre of the wide bay known as the Datu Bight, was Kuching, the major port and seat of the Rajah's government. Across the island, in its river-crossed reaches, was a mixed racial population, including Chinese, Malay and the native peoples – notably the Dyaks – who formed the bulk of the Rajah's forces.

How this place came to be an independent state with its own rajah is best explained by looking at the life of the first rajah, and Harry explains this very clearly. The first rajah was James Brooke, who was born near Bath in 1803. He was employed by the East India Company as a young man, injured and invalided home to England. In a ten-year period he gradually expanded his knowledge and horizons in a range of travelling expeditions, and finally, in 1838, set off for Borneo in his own vessel. Harry explains what happened next:

> The country was a dependency of Brunei in North Borneo, and Rajah Muda Hassim, the Sultan's viceroy, implored the traveller to assist him to restore order amongst his unruly subjects, which the Englishman, with his well-armed yacht and crew of picked men, was able to do. Having communicated with Brunei, the native rajah was empowered to sign an undertaking that, as soon as the rebellion was quelled, the Sultan of Brunei should forthwith appoint the European absolute ruler of Sarawak.

That happened, and within a short time, the new, settled and orderly Sarawak was under the rule of James Brooke, first Rajah. The whole enterprise was a remarkable success. There was a realization of exactly what riches lay in that island; there were natural resources that would yield a very healthy focus of new trade. Security was important, of course, as there were always threats of rebellion and attempts at violent coups from minorities. Harry points out that the government was strengthened 'by the acquisition of European officers, an armed Malay force, and two or three gunboats.'

As it turned out, young Harry, the *aide de camp*, was to be initiated in war when he joined Charles, who had become Rajah in 1865, as he went with his brother-in-law on some expeditions inland. Charles Brooke had been very active in the years just before his rule began, leading an expedition against the Dyaks in 1863 and building a fort at Simanggang in 1864. He had had to cope with a major incursion of Chinese rebels as well, and he undoubtedly made his reputation in the suppression of that problem. Harry explains that on that occasion, the Dyaks (the most skilled fighters in Sarawak) were then fighting for Charles: 'The fierce and warlike Dyaks, led by the young Brooke, were on the track of the fugitives [the Chinese]. ... Finally, and after terrible hardships, about 600 exhausted Celestials contrived to reach Sambas, in Dutch Borneo, these being the only survivors of a force of over 6,000 men.'

Naturally, this success served to reinforce the position of power and authority the Rajah now enjoyed. Later, in his days as a journalist, Harry wrote a piece on Charles Brooke, with the aim of explaining for British readers at home how the government in Sarawak worked. He quoted Charles as saying:

> Trust in my people is the great safeguard of my position. It is easy to govern a country with warships and 12-inch guns, but I have none of these resources. ... I prefer to govern my natives without them. ... I am accessible to all, and the people come to me at any hour of the day. Malays, Dyaks, Hindoos [Hindus], Chinese, men, women and children, all come, convinced that they will receive justice at my hands.

Charles Brooke's background and experience were indeed very impressive. He was born in 1829, and joined the navy in 1842, and his first commander was none other than Willes Johnson in command then of the *Wolverine*. After that initial experience, he was midshipman on the *Dido*. By 1849 he had worked himself up to being senior mate on the *Terrible*. He joined the Sarawak service three years later.

As for young Harry, soon to become familiar with Sarawak life, he wrote extensively about the place, and in his writing we have a foretaste of his style. As a travel writer, he prioritized the civilized, cultured elements in any location; he was always interested in hotels, restaurants, transport or local manners and beliefs. His attempt to understand and explain life in Sarawak shows this very well, as he writes with a readable balance of social commentary and personal reflection on experience. At the heart of his power as a writer is his account of the material world of the communities he explains. Throughout his work on Sarawak, his admiration for the Dyaks is evident, and his description of their habitat is typical:

They are wooden, palm-roof buildings, 70 to 80 feet long, on posts 30 to 40 feet high, and as many as twenty or thirty families sometimes live in one dwelling. … You enter with difficulty by climbing up a notched wooden pole. … The flooring is of split bamboo, with numerous holes through which, if not careful, you may easily slip into the mud and filth below.

During his stay, Harry experienced the warlike eastern peoples and came to confront some of the rebels. Fortunately, he always had the protection of numbers: Brooke had gathered a corps of European officers and gentlemen around him as a central security measure, adopting the usual imperial practice of disciplining and maintaining native fighters in his service. Harry came to know these Dyak tribesmen and their expertise in small arms and in direct combat.

Harry set out on his writing career in Sarawak, as his sister notes. He fastened on to the fact that in travel writing, readers want to sense and experience the danger that the writer felt in an alien, unfamiliar place. Hence, a typical de Windt narrative is one in which the writer is constantly being tested: his books depend on discomfort, unpleasantness and downright horror at times, all being presented through a tough but cultivated sensibility. Hence, in Sarawak he has to mention and describe what the European reader would surely be most intrigued by – headhunting culture. He does not disappoint:

I only once attended a head-feast, held after a great victory, which took place in a house containing several hundred inmates. The proceedings lasted for three days, during which the incessant beating of drums and gongs rendered sleep impossible. A score of recently decapitated heads were suspended from a beam in the centre of the house, and these were smoked over a slow fire until the skin assumed the consistency of leather.

The Sarawak experience was arguably an education in itself – from the school of life. But he still had seniors and guides who took an interest in a young man's career. It was decided that he should have some more traditional educational experience, with the aim at first of joining the army. But Harry's true education was to be centred on his massive appetite for life and his determination to learn from people and places, rather than from books. Sarawak had given him a taste for adventure and it was never to leave him. As will be seen, the experience gave him the material for his first book, at least in part.

Meanwhile, the Chancery guardians had further plans for Harry. In *My Restless Life* he gives a vivid and racy account of his wild life as a Cambridge undergraduate, which ended in 1876, the year his brother George died.

At first, on return from Sarawak, the plan was to have him sit the entrance examinations for the army; the system was for all candidates to sit a general paper, and crammers (usually based in London) were employed for this purpose. Harry never tried to claim that he was at all interested in academic study, and he hated the notion of concentrated study for examinations. Fortunately for him, his fellow students were not in the mood for work either, and so he and this group savoured the delights of London, and Harry took the first steps in his life as a horseman and race enthusiast.

He locates this life of pleasure firmly in the early 1870s, which was for him a golden age, particularly as it centred in his beloved Paris. In London, he and his friends enjoyed the theatre and the gaming rooms above all, with a little physical exercise such as boxing or rowing in between the frisks and fancies. He wrote:

We could do pretty much as we liked at Clapham … and spent most of our afternoons in London. …The Criterion had then just been opened and they would spend long hours at its glittering bar, talking to the doll-like barmaids, consuming countless bottles of pale ale, and trying to look as if they enjoyed it.

It was the time when the theatres were booming in London; legislation had been passed to allow lesser, fringe theatres to stage dramas as well as have music, song and sketches. It was also the heyday of the music hall, and Harry and friends chose the Oxford as their favourite. It was on Oxford Street, and just before Harry arrived in town, there had been a serious fire there – in February 1868. But by 9 August 1869, it was reopened. It was run by the great impresario Charles Morton, and historian Christopher Pilling has described what was on offer: 'At Morton's Oxford there was a proper stage, but in the main body of the hall, with its brilliant gas lighting, the restaurant element continued … the bars and barmaids were also a feature. Morton revived the part-singing and operatic elements of the earlier tavern concerts.' There was also Evans's Music-and-Supper Rooms in Covent Garden, which Harry and friends enjoyed, along with much lower establishments, which Harry does not describe in detail. But Frederick Wellesley, later military attaché in St Petersburg, was one of Harry's contemporaries, and he too was a regular at the 'dives' of the time in the city. He wrote in his memoirs:

> They were called Night Houses and were most of them situated in streets in the neighbourhood of the Haymarket. … There were other haunts of a still lower description which the *jeunesse d'orée* [gilded youth] of London used to frequent. One public house was kept by Jimmy Shaw, in the back premises of which were pits for cockfighting, dog fighting, badger baiting and rat killing. The smell of this place was unbearable, and its attractions not very great.

At this time, almost everyone seems to have met Arthur Orton, the infamous 'Tichborne Claimant', who had gone on trial to determine whether or not he was an impostor trying to claim the vast Tichborne family fortune and was then involved in his second trial, which was to end in February 1874. This was one of the most dramatic and momentous criminal trials in British history. It took the presiding judge a month to offer his summing-up to the court. Harry and friends met

Orton. Harry wrote, 'We used to visit him at the Waterloo Hotel in Jermyn Street, where he generally received us in a kind of snuggery behind the bar.' It was a significant experience in Harry's life, as his interest in criminology was to burgeon as his experience and travel progressed. Not only was he to become a leading authority on Russian prisons, but also, he became a member of the Crimes Club, with Arthur Conan Doyle, as will be explained in chapter 7.

His passion for criminal studies began with people (the Tichborne Claimant was not the only villain he met) and that is significant; it did not begin with anything that may be called academic or theoretical. This interest burgeoned at a time when there was a desire for criminology to become more professional. Methods had been conceived that would transform police work, and although fingerprinting was not applied and made use of by Scotland Yard until 1900, prisons and police work were being modernized and streamlined in the 1870s. When Harry later came to be seen as an authority on penology, he would have that early experience of actually meeting and studying criminals face to face. He took every opportunity to enter a jail and make notes. Even in tiny Montenegro, during his trip in 1905, he visited the women's prison at Cettigne, commenting, 'The women's prison resembled an almshouse, with open doors, in and out of which they strolled unwatched and uncontrolled, although the warder … gravely pointed out an imaginary boundary beyond which they were "requested not to go".' Even Harry, who had seen the insides of prisons across the world, was stunned and amazed at the liberality and forward thinking regime in that small jail.

Harry had a first taste of European travel at this time – in the mid 1870s – and it was then that there was a war brewing between Russia and Turkey. Wisely, he did not venture that far eastwards, going only as far as Vienna and Budapest. Harry was at Magdalene College at this time, and his journeys were merely one element in a rather wild life. He and his friends typify the 'young blade' stereotype, out for any kind of adventure, and everything fuelled by heavy drinking. He expected Vienna to be teeming with possibilities and excitement, but his conclusion was, 'I have always found it a most depressing city … and yet there seems to be a prevalent idea in England that Vienna is one of the gayest cities in Europe.' He soon moved on to Budapest, and then to Orşova.

This is important, because it shows Harry's taste for the wild side. When he and his student friend boarded a steamer to Orşova, a small-scale adventure began. This means that there was fear and apprehension. He recalled in *My Restless Life*, 'We had a miserable journey of about four days, in a small, comfortless boat, crowded with so-called Russian patriots on their way to help their Servian brethren repel the Turk. ... Some were cavalry officers and others wild-eyed Cossacks, armed to the teeth.'

Orşova was also a disappointment, and one wonders whether Harry and friend were not, in effect, eager to move to the boundaries of the war. But they did not need to shift from the town to find the excitement they sought: they joined a party of drinkers, and as matters intensified, suspicions were aroused. Harry explains what happened next:

> We walked in the middle of the road, keeping a sharp look-out, but when it came the attack was so sudden that we were taken completely unawares. Only the German carried a revolver, which he was too drunk to use, while to shout for the police would have been useless. ... These thoughts flashed through my mind as I felt my throat violently encircled from behind, while poor L———, struck with a stick on the back of the head, lurched heavily forward and fell on his face in the snow. Smith luckily dodged his man ... and was able to deliver a smashing blow full in the eyes of my assailant.

When the group moved on the next day to Constantinople, the Russo-Turkish War was over.

In 1877, Harry was twenty-one, and he obtained his allowance from the family annuity. He was a young man of independent means, and he notes that this enabled him to 'carry out certain minor projects of travel which eventually led to important journeys of exploration.' In other words, his career was being conceived and planned, in spite of other distractions, and these were many. At this point in life, his time was taken up with travel, drinking, encountering the criminal side of sub-cultures around him, and occasionally also, gambling, in a small way. But there was something else: he had a passion for horse racing, and he was to become for a short while a jockey, and then an owner, in the 'Sport of Kings'.

He started to attend race meetings around London when he was a student, so this meant visits to Windsor and other small courses. But he writes in *My Restless Life* that his interest was not in the betting side, but in riding. He explains, 'My great aim in life was to ride a race, but this seemed to be an unattainable ambition until the winter of 1878.' The opportunity came while he was at a house party, and there was then an 'open steeplechase', which meant that gentlemen amateurs could enter and ride. He found that there was a choice of mounts, and he picked 'a venerable but speedy mare belonging to a young farmer near Cambridge'. The horse was called Folly, and he had to pay £10 for the ride. He managed to ride the horse – a rank outsider – into third place.

Harry now had the thrill of riding in his veins, and he was next in the saddle in Cheshire. But he knew full well that there were risks, mainly because it was strictly an illegal meeting, meaning that it was run outside the racing rules as established at Newmarket or the Grand National (flat and chasing rules respectively). The result was a dangerous escapade. He recalled in *My Restless Life*, 'There was a big field, and the course being a cramped one, with a dangerous turn, I was jostled at the latter and nearly came a nasty cropper.'

This was a hard lesson learned, and he switched to try to work in more respectable racing circles. He took part in setting up a small stud, and acquired much more time riding to become more skilled at the art. Success was slow in coming, but he was working with men who knew the turf better than he, and on a mount called Holstein, they won two races at Worcester. He was working on the very slender margins of the sport in England, but he was always going to have a knowledge of France, and later, after the Great War, his turf activities extended across the Channel.

Harry for a time mixed in some of the most important racing circles; he mentions, for instance, his friendship with Garret Moore, who rode a Grand National winner, The Liberator. He spent a few years riding at minor provincial courses, and gradually came to see that there was no future in that, and his days as a crazy student, in a college that at the time did not seem to care too much about academic distinction in its ranks, were numbered.

Basically, he was lost and in need of being pushed in the direction of a career, but there is no doubt that Harry was a 'square peg' – he was always meant for working against the grain, going his own way. For all his love of society, he was the ideal candidate for the profession of individualist. He was, paradoxically, a lone wolf who also needed periods in which he joined the pack.

Chapter 3

First Travels

But for me, all the East is contained in that vision of my youth. It is all in that moment when I opened my young eyes on it.

Joseph Conrad, *Youth*

Some periods in British history immediately exhibit to the historian a restlessness, a need in the people to achieve, to see other lands and learn from other places and people. The Victorian age had this, perhaps most strongly expressed in Tennyson's poem, *Ulysses*:

> *I cannot rest from travel: I will drink*
> *Life to the lees: all times I have enjoyed*
> *Greatly, have suffered greatly, both with those*
> *That loved me, and alone ...*

It was a poem that expresses the need, even for older people, to maintain the vision of achievement and a search for knowledge and experience. In the early nineteenth century, much of this urge had been a second stage to the Grand Tour, in which knowledge was gathered along with the artefacts. But there was also the amassing of knowledge from across the empire. Before the 1870s, there had been a massive body of cultural and topographical knowledge of the many states and territories of the British Empire, but this knowledge was recorded in such things as learned journals and was often the work of gentleman enthusiasts and dilettantes. Many of these were officers, men who had learned several Indian languages, for instance, and had spent their leisure time gathering information that would be potentially of real value in a wartime situation. But essays on anthropology and basic

maps of trade routes or drawings of tombs and temples were not easy
to catalogue for military purposes. On the other hand, it is a simple
matter for historians today to look at the numerous small wars in the
nineteenth century, all across the globe wherever the map was red for
empire, that more knowledge of such people as Maoris or Zulus would
have helped the situations a great deal. When the intelligence
department finally arrived, the priorities were maps and languages.
But it was also recognized that there was latent value in simply
gathering and ordering a huge amount of information, mainly
geographical and geomorphological. It was decided, fifty years after
Wellington had written home to buy a map, that something should be
done to make such desperate measures obsolete.

Travel in the nineteenth century was very much under the
influence of wars. After the Battle of Waterloo, travel for British
people began to change from the educational and dissolute Grand Tour
to the voyage of real adventure. *The Westminster Review* in 1816
explained, 'When peace came … when our island prison was opened
to us, it was the paramount wish of every English heart, ever addicted
to vagabondizing, to hasten to the Continent.' Then, after the Crimean
War of 1853–56, the horizons expanded still more, and the East
beckoned. Harry de Windt, as an adolescent, gathered all the required
motivation to travel at just the time when everything pointed to the
age being 'interesting' in the sense of eventful – and a mite perilous
for anyone bold enough to venture overseas.

Historians of travel writing in the nineteenth century have tried to
discern trends and changes of emphasis and intention in the writers
generally; by the time of Harry's first book, *On the Equator*, in 1882,
the nature of travel writing and the reasons for the works in the genre
being written show a mixed bag of material. For instance, at that time
there was still the aim of providing knowledge for the reader at home
about the empire and about other distant, unexplored regions. But
changes were on the way, as the genre attracted more sophisticated
and more complex practitioners. However, literary style never
interested Harry much; he was interested in a plain, but dramatic story.
For him this was a melange of excitement and documentary detail. He

was always drawn to the notion of a quest – a response to a personal challenge to achieve something, or at least, a test of one's mettle. But the topic does run deeper: by the 1880s, to travel beyond Europe was to be part of what might be called the unofficial imperialism of the British. When writers and adventurers went to the unknown regions of the world, it was still a major event, and it was still a part of the global economic and cultural enterprise that had expanded the British Empire, alongside military activity. Henry Morton Stanley, for instance, when he came to England to give a series of talks in 1890, was the subject of several main features in periodicals such as *The Graphic* and *The Illustrated London News*.

Even more fundamental in terms of Harry's travels was the status and purpose of the Royal Geographical Society, which had been founded in 1830. This became almost an adjunct of government, such was its status, and the tradition developed of travellers giving lectures on their travels to the RGS before their material was published commercially. Harry became a Fellow, and he was a part of the grand new enterprise that took travel writing seriously – something that was acceptably serious and scientific work.

Publishing in general still took an interest in producing and mediating works of travel. As Roy Bridges has written, in a study of travel in this period, 'Among the publishers who fed the enormous pubic interest in popular travel works, John Murray was probably the leader. His links with Murchison [a geologist and RGS leading light] and the RGS were close. Stanford was also important in this field. Edinburgh, with Blackwood and two specialist geographical and educational publishers, Johnson and Bartholomew, was able to rival London.'

Harry was also entering the profession of authorship at a time when periodical publishing was burgeoning, largely in response to the new mass readership of clerks and commuters into London, who were eager for self-development and learning under the influence of the new gospel of self-help and social aspiration promulgated by John Ruskin and others.

Before setting off for his first sustained journey, Harry still had some domestic adventures; apart from his exploits in the world of

31

horse racing, he had a more civilized, comfortable jaunt, probably to start some experience of more lengthy travel. This was a sea journey to China by way of Australia. He was, as a youth, prone to accidents, and was often injured, either from sporting exploits or from high jinks while on the loose with his peers in the early hours; he could sow his wild oats with the best of the young roués in his college and in the racing fraternity, and limbs were broken. This first journey relates to this life, as he explains in *My Restless Life*:

> I think I may say that my passion for wandering about the world was first brought about by an accident. ... The result is that, to this day, my right arm is considerably shorter than the other, and at that time, complications set in. Thus I was compelled to give up race-riding ... and travel seemed to me the most pleasant and profitable mode of passing the time.

He decided on taking advantage of the Thomas Cook provision for those with wanderlust. After the beginnings of the Cook enterprise in the Midlands in the 1840s, the firm had grown by the late 1850s into the first package tour business, taking travellers into Europe. Cook obtained the co-operation of the main railways across France and Switzerland, and he soon learned what was required in order to pre-plan holiday excursions for the new middle classes in England, eager to see the world beyond their provincial experience. By the 1880s, this business had extended into sea voyages across the world, based on the same principle, so that Harry aimed to travel as far as Melbourne, but then move on elsewhere, off the Cook itinerary. He had a friend who ran a sheep farm in New South Wales.

On this first jaunt, Harry had an experience relating to one of his heroes. Throughout his writings, there are several notes about his heroes; he relished the lives and works of those men of action who combined art and creativity with adventure and derring-do. One of these heroic figures was the Australian, Adam Lindsay Gordon, who was renowned as both jockey and poet, so it is not hard to see the reasons for Harry's interest in him.

Gordon was born in the Azores in 1833, and had been sent home to England for his education. Here he had not done well, in spite of his friendships, notably that of the great Gordon of Khartoum (who was no relation). But like Harry, academic study was not for him, and Adam was sent out to Australia, where he was to become something of the 'wild colonial boy' in the old song. He took an interest in horse racing and became a jockey, but also wrote popular narrative poems, one of his most successful being *The Ride from the Wreck*, which related to a shipwreck. In 1864 he accomplished something that Harry would really admire – a daring leap on the edge of Blue Lake, and this is explained on the obelisk that was erected later: 'Gordon made his famed leap on horseback over an old post and rail guard fence onto a narrow ledge overlooking the lake, and back again.'

His fortune then declined somewhat but he moved to Victoria and there he became the jockey that Harry would have read about at that time. As a poet, he was to enlarge his reputation even more, publishing *Bush Ballads and Galloping Rhymes*, which is highly rated in the history of Australian literature. In June 1870, he shot himself, largely down to the stress of his penniless state. In 1857 he had met the Reverend Julian Woods, and their friendship was literary, with Woods taking an interest in his new friend's poetry. We can imagine Harry's thrill when he met this Father Woods, and he provides a cameo of the man:

> The Father had ridden many a hundred miles, and spent many months alone in the bush, with Gordon, who never moved without a well-worn copy of Homer in his pocket. For Gordon's classical knowledge was only equalled by his marvellous horsemanship, and his famous verses, entitled *How We Beat the Favourite*, will probably never be surpassed as a sporting poem, in the English language.

His other significant encounter out in Australia was with Ned Kelly's sister, Kate. Ned, who had been killed in late June 1880, was very much the talking point across the continent when Harry arrived, was styled the Bandit of Glenora, and Harry's comment on meeting Kate was, 'Miss Kelly was rather proud of her brother's achievements and had invented a fiery cocktail known as a "Glenora" as a tribute to his memory!'

On the last stretch of this outward journey, to China, Harry became acquainted with some people who were seasoned travellers for God – the missionaries who went out to the Far East in considerable numbers at the time – but he had little comment to make on them. He was far more interested in Hong Kong, noting that, 'Hong Kong is one of the few places in the world where you need never feel bored, if only for the fact that there are numerous places to get away to – Canton … or Macao, the "Monte Carlo of the Far East".' But there was a fearful experience awaiting him – the cholera.

Harry recalled, in *My Restless Life*, a disturbing sidelight on this terrible disease and its effects, when he had a brush with death: 'The disease was of so virulent a type, that I lunched one day near a man at the club, and, returning from a drive in the evening, saw a hearse awaiting him at the door of his office.'

He returned to Europe via Cairo and was soon feeling well enough to set off on the trip that would provide material for the first book. It was a return to Sarawak. He sets the scene at the opening of the book:

> It was on the 13th of April, 1880 that, accompanied by an old college friend … I left London for the Eastern Archipelago, via Marseilles and Singapore, our destination being Sarawak. … On the evening of the 13th April, we stood on the platform of the Charing Cross Station, awaiting the departure of the mail train for Dover and – our luggage duly registered for Paris – we ensconced ourselves in a smoking carriage, and lit up the fragrant weed, not sorry that we were really off at last.

This was to be typical of Harry's journeys – to be accompanied by a friend (he does not name who, on this occasion) and sometimes by two friends, but never more. He explains the outfitting and preparation, which on this first journey included a cholera belt (a belt for the new vaccine kit invented by Haffkine) as well as a smoking jacket.

In 1880 the journey was a return to his first destination, and in writing about Sarawak, this time he provides more of a factual, documentary account. The reader can feel here the style of the future author of features for periodicals such as *The Wide World*. He has a clear notion of the geography of the island in his mind, and he has enough ethnographic knowledge to explain the basic demography; but on top of this he cannot resist the lure of an exciting tale. The book begins with an explanation of the voyage, and he stresses the sheer human noise and confusion: 'The hubbub and the noise were deafening, for the squeaking of some sixty or seventy pigs, which were being hoisted aboard a vessel alongside, bound for Barcelona, added to the din, and combined to make what the French would call *un vacarme infernal.*'

Sailing on the *Sindh*, he was amongst a mixed group of races, and he took pleasure in noting that one of his favourite stereotypes was on board: 'I christened him The Inevitable ".....".' He was the standard know-all who has seemingly travelled the entire world and seen it all. He will be encountered again on Harry's journeys.

But Sarawak is at the centre of the book, and Harry begins with the capital, Kuching. However civilized this might be, it is the wild, little-known world that impinges on Harry's consciousness: 'Riding and driving are but still in their infancy, and Kuching boasted of only some dozen horses and four carriages.' But, as with all Harry's books, there is always, somewhere, a little survival of comfort and homeliness, and he takes the reader into this atmosphere with relish:

But the most interesting and novel sight in Kuching is its bazaar, which is built in arcades a la Rue de Rivoli, the shops therein belonging chiefly to Chinamen. ... Birmingham and Manchester furnish these emporiums to a large extent, the article finding most favour with the natives in the edible line being Huntley and Palmer's biscuits.

35

His first travel book is largely a guide, with his own personal touch, the explanation of first-hand experience, and one of his real strengths as a writer is seen here – the material sense of being there, of trying out the native cultural habits and recreations. In this case, this was the experience of the local fauna:

> But the true curses of Sarawak are the rats. Go where you will, avoid them as you may, there is not a bungalow that is not infested with them, and boots, shirts and even cigars, suffer in consequence, and they sometimes make such a noise as to keep one awake for the greater part of the night. ... These pests occasionally migrate at night in large numbers, several hundred of them on one occasion passing through the Rajah's bedroom at Astana on one of these nocturnal expeditions.

But of course, Harry being a man with a taste for danger and for facing a challenge, he and his friend have to go across Sarawak to a more testing atmosphere. They went to Matang, which involved a climb, accompanied by a 'Mr H', who was formerly an agent on the coffee estate there.

Sarawak at this time was composed of six areas, and these were named residencies, following the system of the East India Company in India. Harry now ventured to the Rejang residency, which had 'the largest and most important river in Sarawak, having five fathoms for a distance of over 130 miles'. As Harry explained, several different ethnic groups lived along that river, with the Dyaks being the majority, numbering around 40,000 people.

Harry and friend sailed on a gun boat, the *Aline*, going from Kuching to Sibu; after that, they planned to venture further into the interior, going 200 miles to Kapit. They took a small launch from Sibu and sailed up the Rejang River. He describes the next stage:

> We arrived off the mouth after a pleasant run of seven hours along the coast and entered the river Rejang, which is here 4 miles broad. ... We anchored off Sarikei, a lonely looking

place, 20 miles from the mouth, consisting of four or five tumbledown Malay houses on a mud bank, and started next day at daybreak, reached our destination at ten o'clock am.

Harry and friend were now at Sibu, and here he was to spend time in the headhunting society, which existed around the Resident's fort and bazaar. The stronghold was Fort Brooke, garrisoned by sixteen Malays, with the Resident and staff living in quarters well off the ground, and reached by high ladders. The Resident asked Harry and friend to dine one evening, and here Harry made a note of the formidable environment:

Our guide firs pointed with evident pride to the bunch of smoke-dried human heads (thirty in number) that were hanging from a post in the ruai [a tribal building], but hastened to assure us, on our examining them very closely, that they were all old ones, the Kanowits having a great dread of being suspected of headhunting.

There were further sights on the trip that served to confirm the European-centred views of such places as 'barbarous' and this was the case in spite of the fact that the government of Sarawak was in the hands of an enlightened British ruler. The fact is that the Rajah retained the attitude of live and let live when it came to custom and tradition. For instance, Harry – being always interested in crime and law – gave an account of an official execution. He notes that in Sarawak he saw a criminal being taken to Batavia, where he would be executed, and he quotes a Malay account of how this was done with the use of a *kris* – a long, sharp sword:

The criminal is led to the place of execution and squats cross-legged on the ground, chewing *penang* [betel-nut] and smoking until the last moment. The *kris* used … is about 16 inches long by 2, broad and quite straight. Grasping this weapon in both hands, the executioner steps up behind the prisoner and thrusts it up to the hilt between the left shoulder blade and neck of the victim. The heart is pierced immediately.

By the end of July 1880, Harry was sailing for Europe, and he was in Cairo, boarding a ship for Gibraltar and then home, by the first days of August. *On the Equator* provided Harry with his first taste of authorship, and it was writing with familiar content, although he did see something of Java and Hong Kong. So his horizons were expanding. But there was something much bolder brewing in his imagination.

After the Sarawak trip, came *From Pekin to Calais by Land*. He refers to this as his first 'expedition' and indeed, compared to the Sarawak trip, this is a prolonged ordeal, something that established what was to become his hallmark as writer and explorer: a need to go to extremes, in every sense. After this trip, he wrote:

> On reaching England I published an account of the journey but the work was necessarily so voluminous that one day poor Dick Grain, the famous entertainer, on being asked if he knew me, replied, 'You mean the little man who writes big books?' Anyhow, this gave me a start in the literary line, for I sold the mss to Messrs Chapman and Hall for a substantial sum, and *From Pekin to Calais by Land* soon ran into a second edition.

The first edition was published in 1889. His fate now was to become the fount of wisdom on the Russian prison system, as his appetite for things Siberian had been whetted.

He was certainly not the first independent traveller to China and other Far Eastern destinations. In addition to the missionaries, there had been the intrepid woman adventurer, Ida Pfeiffer, for instance, who had ventured to China, Singapore and India back in 1846–48. As one historian of travel has written, 'She was an unaccompanied woman; she was perhaps the first European woman to see certain places; she had no official purpose ... and she was in India a decade before the Mutiny at a time when unstructured travelling was rare.' By

Harry's time, as he was well aware, there were more established means of travel available, but he took a special delight in planning routes that would stretch across the wild places and test the adventurer to the limits of endurance.

This trip began with a conversation in Hong Kong. Harry recalls in *My Restless Life* how a friend said, 'How curious it is to think … that a man could hire a sampan on this island, cross over there … and walk dry-shod to Paris.' The idea was planted, and Harry fastened on to it, going to the Club library and studying the relevant maps. Here we have the very core of Harry's motivations as a traveller across the wildernesses of the world. He has written that people kept asking him what was the use of such a scheme – going from Pekin to Paris by way of the Gobi Desert and Siberia. There was no Trans–Siberian Railway when Harry dreamed up this crazy scheme, but someone had done it before – a certain Victor Meignan. Harry would have read the first edition, in French, as the trip was published as *De Paris a Pékin par Terre: Sibèrie–Mongolie*, in 1876.

Harry took heart from this work by a kindred soul, writing, 'According to Meignan, success was mainly a question of patience and physical endurance, with which latter, I may say, I have been fairly well endowed by nature.' He spoke to the Russian Consul, and then his friend Lancaster agreed to join him, and the trip was in preparation. They were to follow the routes of the tea caravans and their transport would be basic stagecoaches, with stinky hovels as the only resting places *en route*.

The first place where anything significant happened was at Kiakhta. On a map of 1900, this settlement (now known as Kyakhta, in the Republic of Buryatia) had been reasonably well developed, having a tea bourse (market) since the 1840s, and was about 200 miles south-east of Irkutsk, near the edge of the massive Lake Baikal. The Russian–Chinese border had been fully opened to trade in the 1860s. Harry gives an account of the place as it was in the 1880s: 'Kiakhta is a queer place; an odd mixture of Mongolian barbarism and Russian (or rather Siberian) civilization. The only inn was a hovel, where we occupied a filthy room devoid of furniture.' But Harry and Lancaster were invited to one of the most memorable and testing repasts of Harry's entire career as a traveller. The meal was largely one of alcohol, and lasted for twelve hours. Towards the mid-period of this epic binge, the two Britishers started to wilt, and Harry explains, 'I managed to see the ghastly entertainment out ... but poor Lancaster succumbed about five o'clock in the morning and fell asleep in a chair. Noticing this, the Professor, a black-bearded Hercules, left his seat, took my friend up in his arms full-length, like a baby, tenderly kissed him on both cheeks and laid him full-length on a sofa!'

They moved on to Irkutsk, and here they experienced a total eclipse of the sun. It was the first significant stage on the route that would, a decade later, be planned as the Siberian rail route that went via Tomsk and Omsk towards St Petersburg. The eclipse was terrifying to the locals: 'The streets were full of terrified men and weeping women – the ignorant, superstitious Siberian peasantry. ... It was like the end of the world, but of short duration. In a few minutes the black veil was drawn aside, as if by some giant's invisible hand.'

The journey was straightforward and comparatively uneventful, judged by the horrors and trials that awaited Harry on his later Siberian journeys. Back home, he enjoyed the pleasures of his clubman life among his peers in the arts and the theatre, knowing that he had sold his manuscript and had set himself on his writing career. He was soon restless; he wrote, in *My Restless Life*, 'Our long and adventurous land journey from China to France had inspired me with a taste for ventures of this kind, and I soon wearied of the prosaic life in London.' He quoted some lines of Lord Byron:

> *Thus, as the blemish which cosmetic art*
> *Repels from one, invades another part,*
> *My roving fancy found another vent,*
> *The object changed, but not the sentiment!'*

What does not figure in Harry's memoirs is any account of his personal life. Of course, in that he was no different from his contemporaries; it was not the done thing to air one's dirty linen in public. But, in fact,

Harry was married – the first of three marriages in his life – to Frances Laura Arabella Long, the daughter of Richard Penruddocke Long, who had been High Sheriff of Montgomeryshire and MP for Montgomery. They had been married at St George's, Hanover Square, in July 1882, and they had one child, Margaret Maud, born in 1883. Five years later, Frances filed for divorce on the grounds of desertion, and this went with the claim for the restoration of conjugal rights.

Matters became acrimonious, and Harry charged Frances with adultery. The story was reported in *The Times* on 1 May 1888: something Harry would have hated. At the hearing, Harry, as the report stated, 'offered no evidence in support of his counter-charge, and she having established her charge of desertion, the Court decreed a restitution of conjugal rights.' Harry did not fulfil that demand, and the consequence was that he was guilty of legal desertion. The fact is that he was, of course, travelling the world. But there was also the stigma he acquired with the one bald statement in *The Times*'s report: 'Evidence of Mr de Windt's adultery with a woman whose name is unknown to the petitioner was also given.' A *decree nisi* was awarded, with costs charged to Harry.

The following year was to be a momentous one for Harry. Although he had seen a stretch of Russia's wilderness, he was now to see much more, as his plan was to travel from Russia through Persia to India. In fact, this is precisely the itinerary that had been taken by many of the young political officers of the British Army when they travelled in order to indulge in some espionage, and Harry was involved in this, although he says very little about it. All we have is this enigmatic passage in *My Restless Life*, when he is giving an account of a trip to Egypt:

> I set out alone for the Caucasus, intending to cross the Caspian Sea and reach Calcutta via Bokhara and Cabul [*sic*]. But the Russian authorities at Tiflis would not hear of this interesting itinerary. ... This, by the way, was the first and last occasion upon which I did any work for our Intelligence Department, and since my brief association therewith, I have ceased to

wonder that foreign countries are invariably better supplied with unofficial (but often valuable) information than England.

He was right. Basically, at the beginning of the Great Game in the 1830s, military intelligence meant finding out information by the traditional means: scouts, basic geography, questioning locals and most of all, making sure that there were capable linguists in the regiment. At the heart of the whole enterprise was the officer class, and to understand the achievements of the political officers, it is essential to understand the means by which the officer class communicated, bonded and nurtured that special *esprit de corps* that would pay dividends in battle. One interesting method of gaining an insight into this mindset is to look at the publications of the regiments. For instance, *The Journal of the Household Brigade* for 1871 provides something profoundly important about the army's sense of identity at the time of the Franco-Prussian War in Europe. The journal covers sports reports, lists of brigade masters of hounds, 'the chase and the turf', steeplechasing, pigeon shooting, theatricals, yachting, balls and concerts. Nothing could exemplify the spawning ground of the political officer as well as this: notice that the list of activities represents the enormous gap of time to be filled when an officer was at home, away from the front line of active service. But it was training in disguise: the sport and other personal developmental activities are forming an attitude. With all this in him, all the habits of endurance, teamwork and invention, out in India he would go shooting for weeks, and in between the sport there was 'information', and of course, improvement of spoken Hindi, perhaps.

These officers were to cluster around the more charismatic figures out in the empire, men such as John Nicholson, hero of the Mutiny, and Henry Lawrence, who had a group of protégés for whom he had a special regard and whose careers he nurtured. Charles Allen, historian of the political officers, has defined this 'band of brothers' very clearly:

Such close friendships, between lonely men who lived many miles from each other, finding open expression only in the event of the death of one of their company, were very much the order of the day. This was a brotherhood of young men who shared a vocation: they saw themselves very much as a band of brothers, Paladins at the court of their master and mentor, Henry Lawrence.

Harry, who was still technically a British officer in the 1880s, having been in a militia, would have been ideal for this brotherhood, and as he says, for a short time he was in that body of men. But maybe his independent spirit was too rash for the army. Still, not long before the next trip – mainly across Russia – he had tasted something of the dangers of the Great Game of military intelligence in which Russia and Britain played the espionage gambits across northern India like a game of military chess.

In 1889, then, he was crossing Russia towards India. In Persia, he stayed with Sir Henry Drummond Wolff, the ambassador in Tehran. Drummond Wolff was at that time Minister Plenipotentiary in Persia, and not long before that he had played a very important role in the settlements decided on in Egypt after the revolt of 1882. He was born in 1830, and his mother was a descendant of the great Prime Minister, Robert Walpole. He would have been excellent company for Harry, as he was famed as a storyteller and *bon viveur*. He was also famous at home, as a Conservative, and he was the man who conceived of the creation of the Primrose League, an organization founded in 1883 with the aims of spreading the ideology of 'upholding Queen and Country and the Tory cause'.

Harry went on to Baluchistan, and there he stayed with the Khan at Kelát. He describes his host as 'as cruel and abandoned old scoundrel as ever disgraced a throne, who before he was deposed by the Indian government, had slain thousands of innocent subjects to gratify his passions and cupidity'. Of all the places Harry travelled in, India was not one of his favourites. He wrote, 'I have never cared much for India, and the few weeks I spent there, on this occasion, inspired me with no desire to revisit the country.' He explained this by referring to the vulgarization of the place by crowds of visitors, and he felt the same about the Holy Land, which had also been high on the list of those Europeans who were, in the nineteenth century, extending the boundaries of the conventional Grand Tour, thanks partly to a very influential travel book, *Eothen*, by A.W. Kinglake, published in 1844 with the added title of '*traces of travel brought home from the East*'.

In Harry's diatribe against the new 'package tourists' of the 1880s, we may enjoy an insight into the mind of one who longed for the lonely places, the deserts, of the world. He wrote, of a scene in the Holy Land, for instance, 'Judge ... of my disgust when, after watching a glorious sunset from the Mount of Olives, we sat down to dinner at the hotel, with a party of personally conducted tourists, and it was publicly proclaimed by their leader that ... sandwiches and bottled ale would be served outside the 'Oly Sepulchre.'

Now the first tentative journeys were over, and he was due to have a fateful meeting with Olga Novikoff, but first there is a mystery. Harry, just before returning home, met a certain villain he calls 'Lavine' and he tells the reader that he has only changed one letter of that name from the real one. The first account of a man who is constantly appearing in Harry's memoirs as a Napoleon of Crime is this:

Nikolai Lavine began life as a lieutenant in the Garde de Corps or Russian Life Guards and had ... imperial connections. At this time very wealthy, his reckless mode of life was the talk of St Petersburg. He gave dinners costing £1,000 [£80,000 in today's values] ... within three years of his accession to the family estates, Lavine found himself a ruined man. ... So well did this clever Russian prosper on the bourse and at cards, that he was soon able to rent a fine apartment on the boulevards des Italiens ... he was an expert at extorting money from wealthy women in society.

Who was this man? The identity remains a mystery. But he featured prominently in Harry's life. The first account given in *My Restless Life* ends with this:

> Even at the moment of writing [1908] I read that he has, only last week, for perhaps the fiftieth time, been arrested and tried for obtaining money under false pretences. But the Count will reappear on two occasions, during the course of this narrative … I shall … defer a further account of his iniquitous career until we meet him again.

Certainly, in the context of the Russia of this time, the man of mystery was more than likely one of many in such a society, according to the editors of a study of crime in Russia at the time. They describe it in these words: 'The professionalism and scale of criminality in the nineteenth century were so high that, according to an early twentieth century scholar, there was not an aspect of public life to which the criminal world had not adapted for its own profit.' The strange 'Count Lavine' haunted Harry across the world, appearing like some Moriarty in a succession of unexpected places.

But now one of the few truly formative encounters in Harry de Windt's life was about to happen: he was asked to call at Claridge's Hotel to meet 'Her Excellency Madame de Novikoff'. He adds:

> The name conveyed meant nothing to me, for in those days I took no interest in either home, or foreign politics. And so, that afternoon, I sauntered carelessly around to Brook Street, little dreaming that I was about to visit a lady who had held her own in international controversies with the greatest British statesman of the day, and whose diplomacy and tact had even once averted a disastrous collision between England and Russia.

Olga Novikoff, born Olga Kireev, had been prominent throughout the years of the development of Pan-Slavism in Russia and during the

Russo-Turkish War of the late 1870s. She had attracted to her salon in Brook Street many of the leading writers and thinkers in England at the time.. W.T. Stead, the journalist who had caused a sensation by 'buying' a child to prove how rife the sex trade was in Britain, and who had served a term in gaol for his pains, was a friend of Harry, and it was through Olga Novikoff that Stead and others worked for, as he himself put it, 'the liberation of the Slavs and ... the establishment of good relations between Russia and England. In the face of a public already in the full fierce flush of the Jingo delirium we raised together the banner of the Anglo-Russian alliance.' This crusade had been necessary, many argued, because Britain had been partly blamed for that war between Russia and Turkey. As Stead put it, 'So Lord Beaconsfield was not discouraged from Berlin when he refused to combine to coerce the Turk, and a Russo-Turkish war was the inevitable result. The war cost Russia 100,000 men and £100,000,000. That is the price that Russia had to pay for England's patronage of the Turk.'

Consequently, when Olga Novikoff asked to meet Harry, she was wanting to recruit him in playing a part in that healing of relations between Russia and Britain. But her motives were social and cultural, rather than political. However, as we shall see in the next chapter, perhaps all was not as innocent as it seemed. Harry, reflecting on what had happened at that meeting, summed it up:

> And it was nearing the dinner-hour before I finally took my leave of this kind and gracious lady, who had not only added one to her already long list of friends and admirers, but who had also given me a new object in life. For my connection with the Siberian Exile Question, which has been the one important work of my life, entailing many thousand miles of arduous and sometimes perilous travel, had its origin in that little sunless sitting room, with its huge desk and somber furniture, at Claridge's Hotel in Brook Street.

This meeting is important, because the later charges against him – that he was given the task of 'whitewashing' the prison system – depend on the brief he was given. There is nothing but a literary dimension to the invitation to travel and to write in this meeting, and explanations of how accurate and truthful Harry's Russian reports were will come later, in the next chapter.

Chapter 4

The Prison Expert and Siberia

I know not whether laws be right
Or whether laws be wrong.
All that we know, that lie in gaol,
Is that the wall is strong
And that each day is like a year,
A year whose days are long.
Oscar Wilde, *The Ballad of Reading Gaol*

Olga Novikoff had read about Harry's first Siberian journey, and Harry had noted that on that journey he first saw and learned something of the prison gangs *en route* for Siberia. He wrote, 'in '87, when I came overland from China to France and, during that journey not a day passed that we did not meet prison gangs bound for Irkutsk.' Olga Novikoff had been, amongst many other things, a prison directress in her native country, and she called Harry to the meeting at an important point in the history of the Russian prison system. In fact, this trip was to be the beginning of a long and sometimes bitter feud between Harry and George Kennan. Harry himself explained the situation as it was in 1887:

The good old English legend of men rotting to death in quicksilver mines was the first to explode, seeing that the mineral in question does not even exist in Siberia. And every day brought fresh proofs that, in England at any rate, Siberia as a penal centre had been greatly maligned. Nevertheless, about this time an American traveller, Mr George Kennan, was arousing the indignation of Europe by his lurid descriptions of Siberian prison life in *The Century Magazine*. According to this writer, exiles of both sexes were systematically and grossly maltreated, the gaols and *étapes* [rest stations *en route*] were dens of immorality, filth and disease, and the entire system of deportation was a disgrace to humanity.

By the 1890s, in terms that the modern person would understand, the world was shrinking. As one writer on travel literature has explained:

By 1880 the American Transcontinental Railway and the Trans–Indian Peninsular Railroad had been built, the Suez Canal opened, and that if Jules Verne's *Around the World in 80 Days* was fantasy when published in 1873, by 1890 an American woman journalist, Nellie Bly, had been round the globe in a mere seventy-two.

It is important to clarify the difference between *katorga* and the forced settlers. The latter were technically not in prison, but were in exile; this was different from criminal prison sentences. It has been established that the forced labour system, going back to the eighteenth century, when, in 1722, Peter the Great passed a law to force labour at the Dauriya (or Dauria) silver mines in far Siberia. There had been some kind of eastern exile in Russian society since 1649, when it was thought to be less severe to send people to Siberia than to keep them detained while also mutilating and knouting (flogging) them. In 1736 an Act was passed that enabled estate owners such as the young man in Turgenev's story to dispose of undesirables in the locality. The unfortunate individual would find that his property had been acquired and split up across the community and then he or she was expected to find a home elsewhere; failing that, exile to the east was the only possible next step. Anne Applebuam has pointed out that in the nineteenth century, the numbers of *katorga* workers declined, while forced settlers increased in numbers. She explains: 'In the nineteenth century, *katorga* remained a relatively rare option of punishment. In 1906, on the eve of the Revolution, there were only 28,600 *katorga* prisoners.'

The fact is that the vast areas of Russia to the east of Moscow and the other cities of the Siberian region needed a population, and they had huge natural resources waiting to be tapped for massive profits. Just as Rome had done in her method of having slave colonies established for mining and quarrying, so Russia sent large numbers of expendable people to its Far East. The system did achieve the aim of having a certain level of permanent inhabitants, however, as many exiled forced labour groups did indeed stay. Anton Chekhov met some of these, and he noted, 'The majority of them are financially poor, have little strength, little practical training, and possess nothing except their ability to write, which is frequently of absolutely no use to anybody.'

As the system existed by Harry's time, the established dual punishments of exile to the Russian Far East or convict labour were still the staple of the regime. There had been some changes, however, mid-century: in 1835, there were two locations for exile – in Eastern or Western Siberia. Obviously, those political dissidents exiled to the Western Siberian region were nearer home, and so visits to them were more manageable; there was, in the words of Brian Reeve, the translator of Chekhov's work on Sakhalin, a 'ladder of punishment' existing:

> Sentences sometimes appeared to comprise wholly arbitrary permutations of hard labour, enforced exile, length of sentence and place of residence in Siberia. It may be noted here that the death penalty had been maintained for those who had been sentenced to convict labour in Siberia for murder and who then carried out one subsequent murder or other serious offence.

When Harry arrived in 1890, there were, according to George Kennan, about 18,000 exiles, but Brian Reeve quotes other sources that state that from 1887 to1898, 100,582 people had been exiled.

Travelling to the wilder regions of Russia by Europeans had first really taken off in the aftermath of a real pioneer – John Parkinson. He had travelled, accompanied by only his Oxford tutor, as far as

Tobolsk, before turning south to reach the Caucasus. Before him British travellers had tended to go only as far as St Petersburg. In the early Victorian period, tour guides began to appear covering trips to the cities of the eastern reaches of the empire; the first English travellers' guide to Russia appeared in the 1830s, but not until 1914 did the famous *Baedeker Guide to Russia* appear, thanks in part to Harry and to George Kennan.

Following the old Silk Road, and with a military priority, the work for the Trans–Caspian Railway began in 1879, but the Trans–Siberian railway did not reach completion until 1916, having been started in 1890. It was ten years after Harry's book saw print that the Russian government published a guide to the Siberian railways, and this included almost 400 photos. The Russians wanted tourism to flower in the forbidding Eastern regions. Harry was surely heartened to know that, by the last years of the century, people were cycling across Russia: Robert Jefferson cycled from Warsaw to Moscow in fifty days in 1895. But of course, Siberia was another matter entirely.

With this background in mind, we need to imagine Harry setting out in 1889, first of all with a wider context in mind. It must seem with hindsight that almost everyone was setting out to visit the Far Eastern coast of the Russian Empire. But they were, except for Harry, mostly travelling by sea. The Tsarevich himself, the future Tsar Nicholas II, set out for far Siberia in mid-1890. He covered the distance of about 51,000 kilometres by railway and 22,000 kilometres by sea in just less than 300 days. Joe Crescente, writing about the journey in 2014, explained:

> One major impetus for this trip was Alexander II's decision to establish the Trans–Siberian Railway. He wanted a member of the royal family to be present for the opening ceremony in Vladivostok. … What is indisputable is that the Romanovs wanted to use this trip as a spiritual mission to spread the Orthodox faith among new peoples and territories around the world.

Then there was the fiction writer and playwright Anton Chekhov, one of Russia's greatest writers: his reasons for going to the island of Sakhalin on 5 July 1890 are far more complex. We reach the point now at which Harry's journey is to be described, and then compared to both Kennan's and Chekhov's accounts of the penal system. The first step is to look at the motives of Kennan and Chekhov; Harry's motive is clear, as he was asked by Olga Novikoff to present a documentary account of the exiles and their lives. Still, there is a note of caution here, and it is something that critics of Harry took into account. This is the Russian tendency – beginning in the reign of Catherine the Great as the handiwork of Grigory Potemkin – of using the 'Potemkin Village' ruse. This refers to Potemkin's creation of a fake village, which was built to impress and deceive the Empress as she travelled along the river Dnieper to the Crimea in 1787. It may be an apocryphal tale, but the point is that Harry's critics – those who were to think he 'whitewashed' his account of the penal colonies – had this to fuel their arguments.

But Harry's own explanations of the circumstances of his journey to the colonies presents convincing evidence that he saw scenes that perhaps some officials did not want him to see. He wrote, 'Suffice it to say that I was provided with an Imperial ukase so powerful and far reaching that it enabled me, without notice, to enter and closely examine any place of confinement, at any hour of day or night, throughout the Russian Empire.'

Now it is necessary to trace that Siberian journey, and to weigh Harry's evidence of what he saw alongside that of Chekhov and Kennan. The latter's views are easily summarized. In 1970, the scholar Taylor Stults wrote an account of Kennan for the *Russian Review*, and he was in no doubt that Kennan's pieces in *The Century Magazine* from 1888 to 1891 were a great and honest realistic achievement. Stults summarizes Kennan's conclusions neatly: 'He repeated the message ... the penal and legal system in Russia usually operated in arbitrary fashion, followed procedures rarely found in the more civilized Western world. Alleged political offences were punished severely by imprisonment or exile without benefit of trial.' A typical extract from Kennan's writings is this, an account of one of his most harrowing witnesses:

> Granted for the sake of argument that there are thousands of happy homes in Russia, that the Empire does abound in cultivated and kind-hearted people … what have these facts to do with the sanitary condition of a tumble-down *étape* in the province of Yakutsk, or with the flogging to death of a young and educated woman in the mines of Kara? The balancing of a happy and kind-hearted family in St Petersburg against an epidemic of typhus fever in the exile-forwarding prison at Tomsk is not an evidence of fairness and impartiality.

Kennan had been given the brief, as a commission from the editor, of writing about the Russian government's treatment of its political exiles. His book, *Siberia and the Exile System*, was published in 1891, just as Harry was in St Petersburg preparing to begin his journey, which would be by train, steamboat and horse-drawn transport.

But there is some background to Kennan's stance on attacking the Russian system. When he had gone to Russia earlier, in the 1880s, with a party financed by the Western Union Telegraph, he had been far from critical of Russia. In fact, he had reported positively in the book published after the trip, *Tent Life in Siberia*. After that, as Alex Butterworth writes in his study of the situation at the time, he had been chided for his credulity, and, 'As a consequence, when Kennan secured a commission from *The Century Magazine* to revisit the Tsarist prison camps in Siberia in 1887, he was more thorough in his investigations.' Arguably, one might conclude, he was out on a mission to paint the whole system black.

Harry, setting out for Siberia, would have been well aware of how the Russian prison system was being mediated in Britain. One important influence was a book by Sergei Kravchinsky, *The Career of a Nihilist* (1889), which had a profound influence on the British press. Alex Butterworth sums this up: 'As much as any literary merit the book may have had, though, it was the shocking reports from Russia then appearing in the headlines that ensured its popularity with the circulating libraries that dominated English reading culture.' Kravchinsky had previously written *Underground Russia*, in 1883, which also revealed the world of radical dissent in the suppressed underworld of Russia's dissenting voices.

In the popular publications such as *The Harmsworth Magazine* there were features showing the horrors of the prisons and the convict experience. In 1894, for instance, *The Harmsworth* ran a feature headed 'Escapes from Siberian Prisons – by one who knows them'. The photos to accompany this are a cruel-looking guard branding a knout; an escapee being shot at by guards; a line of tired convicts walking home from the day's work in the mines; and convicts with brands on their foreheads. In an added image (irrelevant to Russian prisons) the reader is shown two men with a board fastened across their shoulders, with just their heads above the board. The caption reads, 'How Mongolian prisoners are kept in durance vile [journalistic hyperbole for hard labour]'. The anonymous writer foregrounds the long treks made by those who run away and have to walk across the taiga and through forests, along with the tales of bands of robbers who attack parties of convicts who march or who have settled somewhere in the middle of the vastness east of Tomsk. In other words, it is a sensational piece, with selected highlights, all created to disturb and outrage the English reader.

Harry, as he gives an account in *Siberia As It Is* of his meeting with Demetrius Kamorski, the Inspector General of the Russian penal system, before setting out to describe the colonies, is confronted with the issues around the debate. Kamorski says, 'The credulity of the English has always amused me. … They will believe an American journalist, but not their own countrymen; I mean so far as the Russian penal system is concerned. What authority have they for the truth of these so-called Siberian atrocities?' Kamorski gives Harry a full explanation of the shortcomings that still unfortunately exist, and his main argument is political and pragmatic: he explains that the Tsar had planned innovations but circumstances stepped in: in 1887 it was the government's aim to scrap transportation to Siberia as it was, and to use the sea routes. Kamorski adds that 'Rome wasn't built in a day. … Bad as the prisons are … I think you will hardly find them "hells upon earth".'

The book covers far more than a report on Siberia; Harry gives an organic narrative of the penal system, starting with the court processes and prisons in Moscow and Petersburg, and then he moves along the route, as it were, moving eastwards. He conceived the book as a travel book with added statistical material and addenda with statements made by specialists and experts. From the beginning, he was aware that the day was not far off when travellers would find the Russian Far East an attainable destination as an extension of the Thomas Cook remit. In fact, in 1900, as Colin Thubron has described so well, there was an alluring dimension to the very idea of being in the Siberian wastes:

> At the Paris Universal Exposition in 1900, visitors crowding into the Palace of Russian Arts could board a lavish replica of the half-completed Trans–Siberian Railway. Each compartment of the *wagons-lits* [sleeping car] was served by a marble-lined washroom with a porcelain bath. … White multi-lingual waiters served caviar and bortsch in the restaurant car, a diorama of Siberia … was wound slowly past the windows in an illusion of snug villages and eternal forest.

Thubron's book, *In Siberia*, evokes very strongly the ambiguity of Siberia – the way it has always existed in a formidable mythology, placed somewhere between a dreamscape of wild beauty and horrendous exile settlements where people freeze to death. There is no doubt that, back in the late nineteenth century, a prison sentence or political exile out in the Russian Far East meant oblivion. It was the equivalent of Britain's Van Diemen's Land (Tasmania) in the sense that, should freedom be attained, the journey home was still formidable – and of course, expensive.

Still, bearing in mind what has been said about the Russian penal system, it should now be added that Harry was travelling to Siberia at a crucially important time in the history of prisons generally.

Throughout the eighteenth century and the first half of the nineteenth, the impact of the Enlightenment had begun to take effect. This great movement promoting notions of a more comprehensive understanding of mankind, with its revisionary philosophical ideas, meant that ideas of freedom and liberty were in the air. In Britain, for instance, prison legislation beginning with Sir Robert Peel's first spell as Prime Minister in the 1830s, had initiated what would become an overhaul of the penal system, culminating in the 1877 reforms that essentially nationalized the gaols. But this was part of a worldwide movement, and Harry was to become a notable figure in this context by the 1890s.

The first landmark in the creation of a more forward-looking attitude to imprisonment was the first International Prison Congress, held in London in 1872. It had been conceived in the United States in the previous year, but in London, at the Middle Temple, in the very heart of the legal institutions, criminologists and prison administrators met with other intellectuals, and the major issues of penal reform were discussed. *The Times* reported the event, summarizing Lord Carnarvon's opening address, and making a point of stressing the aims of the assembly: 'He hoped the Congress might find time to discuss the subjects connected with reformatories, discharged prisoners' aid societies and penitentiaries ... and also that more means should be given for the moral improvement of the prisoner.'

This was an expression of the mood of the times: since the old houses of correction, which were essentially factories mixed with housing for mendicants and drunks, had been replaced by local prisons based on a graded and planned system of reforming rather than simply punishing the offender, there had been much debate about how and why crime occurred. The social sciences were just beginning to be formed and regulated, and criminology was changing to follow the criminal legislation. For instance, in 1868, public executions were abolished, and the 1861 Offences Against the Person Act consolidated and reformed the sentencing rationale of major criminal offences. Along with this came the idea of sentence planning, whereby an offender's prison period would be staged and monitored, aiming at moral reform.

With all this in mind, it may come as no surprise that in 1896, just five years after Harry's prison visits in Russia, the International Congress was held at St Petersburg. The report on this, which carries prolonged explanations of planned Russian reforms, would suggest that what Harry was told by the Director of Prisons in 1891 was indeed the case. This was Kamorski again, and he stressed that the right thinking regarding reform was going on, but that circumstances were against the success of these aims at the present.

The report of the 1896 Congress includes a list of all the reforms stated back in legislation passed in 1863 (no doubt influenced by the end of serfdom in Russia two years previously). These included several items that Harry, Kennan and Chekhov were to see being confirmed when they visited – directives about corporal punishment and the length of time people were kept in halls of detention. To be fair, this legislation, together with further laws created in 1883, did ease the former terrible regime that had existed earlier. As the author of the 1896 report openly admitted, 'Alexander II reorganized the transportation of prisoners on a more human basis. In 1830, this branch of the service was barbarous.'

There is plenty of written testimony that describes this 'barbarous' system, notably in the experience of Fyodor Dostoyevsky, the great novelist, who was involved in the Decembrist plot to assassinate Tsar Nicholas I in 1849. He was led out for execution, and then after experiencing what he thought was the moment of his death by firing squad, he was transported out to a prison at Omsk, where he stayed from 1850 to 1854, followed by forced military conscription out in Siberia. In many ways, in that earlier time, the journey out to the prisons was the worst part of the whole sentence as it entailed very long marches through areas of extreme cold, with little food and clothing, followed by shipping out to the prison towns.

This was the situation in 1891 when Harry set off from Moscow. *Siberia As It Is* begins with an account of the Nihilists in Russia and in Europe, and an account of the assassination of Tsar Alexander II, and this serves the useful purpose of giving the reader some idea of the subject of the political exiles – those he will meet later. Harry then has to wait for his letter from Kamorski, which will give him entry to anything in the penal system he wishes, apart from the exiles. Chekhov was told the same thing, but both Chekhov and Harry found ways to circumvent this order. Then he is on his way, first of all by steamer, and from one of these vessels he has his first sight of prisoners, who are on a barge alongside: 'Are these laughing, boisterous fellows really on their way to Siberia – to the land of despair, desolation and death? Or is all that we have read concerning that mysterious country a clever fiction?'

After more travel towards Siberia, he is finally on the verge of prison country, on board a tarantass, a carriage led by four horses. This vehicle broke down, and Harry's thoughts turned to wolves. The beasts are howling around the tarantass, but Harry notes, 'Tonight the crack of a whip was apparently enough to send them scampering away.'

Eventually, the prison visits begin – the first one being at Tobolsk, which was still more than 2,000 miles from the sea at the far end of the massive stretch of Siberia. At that time, he was on board the steamer *Kosagofski*, and he had the opportunity to be taken by the commander of the unit to inspect the Irtysh prison barge. The drawing of this in *Siberia As It Is* makes it clear that the prisoners are penned into cramped quarters, but that food is given to them and the guards treat them well. This report sets the tone for the rest of the book; for the inspection, there is a doctor, with two guards, as well as Harry and the commander. There was certainly concern for health, and food was no different to that in British prisons at the time. Harry gives more details when he is invited to eat with them:

'Come and taste the soup,' said Galtine [the Commander] as he led me to a group seated in the far corner. Spread out on the deck in front of them were a huge loaf of black bread, a couple of cream cheeses, a box of sardines, some Kalachi [round bread cakes] and a packet of tea … the soup was fairly strong and palatable, though rather greasy. It contained some large but rather tough pieces of meat, barley and cabbage.

Documentaries on prison life, at any time, need to stress what is most important to the prisoners, and that tends to be food and exercise time. Harry understood this, and when he inspected the *peresilni* dispersal prison in Moscow, where prisoners were held until they were despatched eastwards in groups of a few hundred at a time, the dietary was studied, and he includes this for his readers: 'The fare was mainly gruel, dripping, rye bread and small amounts of meat.' Regarding exercise time, Harry was to see, on arrival in the Eastern Siberian gaols, that the Russian system allowed for free movement within the given boundaries in settlements, and these were large.

If we recall the nature of British convict prisons at this time – places such as Dartmoor and Portland – the Russian approach is more impressive in terms of freedom of movement, but, as will be seen, the demands made on labour were terribly severe out in the wilds, where trees had to be cut and lugged to areas where they would be used for building.

Still, when it came to food, health and care, at least on the journey east, the Russian system comes out well in Harry's account.

At Tobolsk, Harry makes a point of lambasting an account in print back home – a work called *The Russians of Today*, published in 1878, and he does this to continue his insistence that the Russian penal system has been maligned and distorted: 'This book … contains much entertaining, if not very instructive matter, dealing with Siberia. The author, however, had never visited the country in question.' Harry then adds, 'It seems a pity, however, that the author should not have confined himself to fiction pure and simple while he was about it.'

When Harry comes to inspect the prison at Tomsk, it is, in today's vocabulary, an 'unannounced' inspection. Harry describes the situation as the governor responds to Harry's pass provided by the director in Moscow: 'He is, as I afterwards discover, a good fellow in the main, and having read my authority, apologizes, "I did not know your permit was so complete … Tomorrow you will see us at our worst."'

Harry proceeds, and continues to dispel the false accounts of the lives of the exiles. At one point he chooses a specific topic that has attracted great interest back home: 'Much has been written concerning

59

the sorrows and sufferings of Polish exiles sent to Siberia after the insurrection by order of the Tsar Nicholas. That prisoners at the mines were then severely, and occasionally cruelly, treated unfortunately cannot be denied. ... There was no properly organized exile system in those days.' In contrast, Harry chooses an example of one of these exiles to present an opposite view, quoting a Polish prisoner's account, which includes a description of a cottage that he lived in, along with other Poles: 'The kitchen stove which baked our bread also warmed an apartment ... used as our sleeping-room and the other, which might be called our salon, was provided with a nice-looking Tartar *ezulan*, or round open fire-place. ... We had employed a Tartar to construct the house for us.'

Integral to the whole system is the *étape* – a small holding establishment along the post road to Siberia, and Harry came to know these well. In *Siberia As It Is* he provides a sketch and a description. The account is mixed, but on the credit side we have this: 'resting places for the night, which, with their bright yellow walls and red roofs, form a distinctive feature in nearly every Siberian village along the great post road.' He makes it clear that the prisoners are segregated, so that there are separate rooms for men, women, political exiles and the escort. That fact alone was progressive at the time. British prisons had, in their 1877 developments, been organized in terms of segregation to avoid what was termed at the time 'contamination' of new offenders by old lags.

Harry was well aware that it was while on the road that the prisoners would be under most duress and would face most demanding experiences – that is, with reference to the political exiles, who would not be doing much hard labour when they arrived. There may have been squalor at the cells and communal halls out at the far camps, but at least when the prisoners left Moscow they had plenty of provisions, such as shirts, drawers, linen, breeches, tunics, a sheepskin pelisse (jacket), caps and gloves. The women had shirts, drawers, petticoats, tunics and greatcoats, along with shoes, gloves and high boots.

There were limits, of course; Harry is not painting a picture of Paradise. For instance, we have this: 'A convict arrives at the *étape* tired out after a long march, and drenched with rain and perspiration. The government provides him with a change of clothes, but no drying appliances. If the weather on the previous night has been wet, he must shiver in wet clothes the long night through.' The basic central accommodation in the Russian system was the common cell room. Anton Chekhov provides a very vivid description of this in his book on the island of Sakhalin:

> Right the way down the middle of the cell stretched one continuous bed-board, with a slope on both sides, so that the convicts could sleep in two rows, with the heads of one row turned up towards the heads of the other. The convicts' places are not numbered, and are in no way separated from each other, and owing to this, it is possible to place between seventy and 170 people on the boards. There is no bedding whatsoever. Either they sleep on the hard surface, or else they lay on torn sacks, their clothing and all sorts of rotting rubbish. ... On the boards lie caps, boots, bits of bread, empty milk-bottles ... under the chests are filthy sacks, bundles, tools.

Like Chekhov, Harry went to Sakhalin. This is the long, thin island off the coast of Siberia, north of Japan. Predominantly, this was for political exiles, and so it had a scattering of small settlements where the intellectuals mixed with the manual workers, and also, settled colonists were part of the mix. It was always the Russian idea to populate the immensity of Siberia with Russians as well as with the people of the eastern races. These were mainly Samoyeds, Koriaks (or Koryaks), Ostiaks (or Ostyaks), Kuriles, Bouriates (or Buryats) and Tungusians (or Tungusics). Harry, not wanting to leave any stone unturned, gives a short account of these various ethnic groups, in order to assure his readers of his thoroughness.

The adventure was, of course, initiated by Olga Novikoff, and whether or not the brief was simply to offer a counter-narrative to that of Kennan and the other authors who had given accounts of 'Siberian horrors', there is no doubt that Harry had to include a specific description of a typical Siberian prison. The subject of whether or not Harry was offering a 'whitewashed' view of the prisons relates to wider issues of the time, and this partly explains why there was such acrimony between Harry and George Kennan. Kennan's strong criticisms of the exile system and the prison conditions in Siberia relates to a general view of Russia. Anthony Cross, historian, explains in his book on British responses to Russian culture in the late nineteenth century:

> British Russophobia continued to be fed by the perceived Russian threat in the Near and Far East and Central Asia, and the manoeuvrings of the Great Game, but it was underpinned to a previously unequalled degree by sympathy for the oppressed. ... Poets joined with novelists to condemn the excesses of autocracy.

He adds, 'This was seen in Algernon Swinburne's *Russia: An Ode* (1890), in which we have, "Night hath but one red star – Tyrannicide,"' and this was written 'to refute the more optimistic view of Siberia and the exile system.' The latter refers to Harry and to another writer called Landsdell, who had made a similar journey to Harry's not long before.

When his critics looked for evidence of Harry's optimistic view of the prisons, they would need to look at his enquiry regarding the central prison at Tomsk. Today, this is close to Tyumen and Yekaterinburg, a little north of the border with Kazakhstan. Then, this was the heart of the post road east. Harry chooses to devote a long chapter to this, and his view reads like a documentary, with a strong visual sense of place, and lots of detail. He creates a sense of drama, as he reports on the cries of a line of sentries, followed by a shout that then prompts the gates to be opened. Then we have a bold, powerful account of the convicts standing in the rain: 'But for the occasional clank of a leg chain, the quickly hushed whimper of a child, you might almost hear a pin drop as Galtine proceeds to call the roll.'

As Harry watched Galtine, the governor, talk to each convict as the men responded to their names being called, there is even some humour; the convicts are all given some kind of direction, and the crowd is asked if there are any complaints. That might seem like the kind of thing that a prison governor might do when he is being watched by a writer who will report on his actions, but again there is humour, until the governor sorts out a situation and makes a judgement from his Solomon-like status. He tells one man that he is lucky to have escaped the 'black cell'.

But anyone at home who thought the book is a propaganda exercise for the government should have read this passage concerning a woman voluntary exile who asked for her son's leg irons be removed: '"He is ill and weak," she sobs, and "Excellency, he is all I have left in the world." The doctor is summoned, and pronounces the lad sound and strong enough to bear the burden.' But then, as Harry explains, 'Galtine is merciful, saying quietly to her, "They will be struck off tonight."'

Harry is well aware of the other important issues concerning the prison establishment. The matter of the prison population, for instance, is dealt with. The prison he writes about at Tomsk is a *peresilni* – a forwarding establishment. As is the situation today with British local dispersal prisons, there is a tendency for overcrowding to become a problem, often because allocating prisoners to the next transfer is a slow business. Harry gathers some facts in this case: 'The Tomsk *peresilni* is constructed to accommodate 2,000 prisoners. It contained, on the day of my visit, 2,176, including voluntary exiles and their children. I was told that ... three years ago, as many as 3,000 convicts were located in the prison.' Now, this has to be one of the main arguments in support of Harry's documentary being a real account of the facts before him. Whitewashing usually plays around with figures.

He goes on to describe the various cells and the communal areas; he measured the rooms and studied the sleeping areas, which were organized in the same way as at the *étape*.

In fact, Harry's account has the ring of truth on a number of occasions, but more particularly in this report, when there is an incident that involved over a hundred new arrivals:

63

The stout, apoplectic little gaoler shouted himself blue in the face, but in vain. His cries of *Smirno!* [attention!] were drowned in the hubbub, and it was only when the noisier spirits at the further end of the room had caught sight of the green and gold uniform that order was restored.

What Harry is doing here is being careful to put things in perspective. He adds, 'It reminded one of a parcel of rowdy boys.' One cannot help feeling that George Kennan would have reported a riot.

The other main preoccupation of all prison inspections is what today is called the 'regime' – the routine, and most of all, the useful work or study being built into the average day. Harry, for instance, concentrates on what work he saw; in the women's *kameras* (communal cells), he gives a neat cameo of the situation: 'The ones I visited contained both criminal and fee exiles. The former rose as we entered and made us a waist bow. Many of the latter were employed, knitting, sewing or washing linen. The children looked clean, rosy and well.'

The topic that always fed the European papers with scandalous and dramatic reports was healthcare. Harry went to the Tomsk hospital and saw cases of smallpox and typhus, and he notes, 'This is usually the black spot of the *peresilni*. But, as usual, I am agreeably disappointed.' He notes a 'large, airy room' and in the supporting kitchens he sees a sound organization, working well. A doctor tells him, 'The death rate is low and there has been no epidemic here for the last fifteen years.'

Finally, there is the question of corporal punishment to be handled. Flogging was in the system, but was not applied randomly. Harry notes that men have been birched, even while he has been there. It has to be recalled that at the time, soldiers in the British Army were still being flogged, and only a generation before Harry's trip, it was not uncommon to find in the papers reports of military flogging that caused the deaths of the victims.

This long documentary account, forming a large section of *Siberia As It Is*, concerns the Goubernski prison. Harry includes a picture of this in the book, and we see a solid, rectangular white building of four storeys, with a surrounding low fence and sentries on duty. It looks far more pleasant than the London gaols in 1890, with their dismal central towers and long, dour halls.

On his return, for the next year or so, controversy raged in the press on the subject of the Russian penal system, and Harry found himself deeply engaged in this interplay of fact and opinion. This raged in London. The man whom we perhaps would have liked to have seen involved was Anton Chekhov, who wrote, on return to the Western Russia of intellectuals and art: 'While I was living on Sakhalin, I experienced only a certain bitter taste deep inside me, as if from rancid butter, but now, in retrospect, Sakhalin appears to me to be utter hell.'

In the midst of the controversy, Harry gave lectures, and sometimes he was interviewed. He spoke to *The Pall Mall Gazette*, for instance, in January 1894, and this was reported with the headline 'Do Siberian Horrors Exist?'. His interviewer went straight for the jugular, when Harry told him that he intended to go next to Sakhalin, 'where no Englishman has been allowed to go.' The interviewer responded with, 'Except Mr Kennan?' And Harry's reply sums up the overall attitude he had to his opposition: 'Oh no, Mr Kennan hasn't been there. I go there, more or less, by invitation of the Russian government.' The interviewer then asked the question that all his readers would have wanted to ask: 'How do you come to be on such good terms with the Russian government?' Harry's reply was to explain the meeting with Olga Novikoff.

It was *The Spectator* that took up the cudgel on behalf of Kennan. On 13 August 1893, it ran a feature on the subject, with this questioning of Harry's statements made to the press earlier in the controversy:

> he means to impute to Mr Kennan, first that he had described a certain prison at Tomsk which he had never seen, and secondly, when he had to drop that insinuation, that Mr Kennan had purposely misdescribed the prison which he had seen. This sort of thing rather defeats its purpose, for the critic

who finds Mr Harry de Windt admitting that he founded his insinuation on the mere fact that he asked a single subordinate gaoler in the prison in question when Mr Kennan visited it and was told 'he never visited it at all' becomes rather sceptical as to the value of Mr Harry de Windt's own judgement.

Partly as a result of works such as Harry's, expressing the alternate view to that of Kennan, by 1900 the knowledge of Siberia being mediated reflected the latest thinking, and it seems as though some of the work of the International Prison Congress had had some effect. In *Harmsworth's History of the World*, for instance, published in 1907, the summary of the situation at that point, when the railway had arrived, shows an understanding of the system and of the difference between prisoners, settlers and political prisoners:

> There is apparently a wish to abandon the very dubious method of populating the country by settlements of criminals or political suspects. In the year 1899, Tsar Nicholas II invited a commission to give an opinion as to the advisability of discontinuing transportation to Siberia. ... This is the beginning of the end of a practice which has given an unpleasant aspect to the character of Siberian colonization. ...
> The further destinies of the exiles concerned nobody; the majority probably died there.

The writers were not to know what lay in wait after the 1917 Revolution, of course, which brought the beginnings of the Gulag system. But as Russia entered the twentieth century, at least some of the claims made at the 1896 Congress had been made good.

However, as time went on and Harry, having been divorced, as previously noted, found himself in a situation in which he wanted to return to Siberia. It was not long after that he was to meet the woman who was to be his second wife, Hilda Frances Clark. But in the meantime he was still free to follow his latest project. He had told the press this, and in 1894 the Russian government invited him to go to

Sakhalin, where Chekhov had so recently been. Harry knew nothing of Chekhov's work, and never mentioned the great writer, but he knew that Sakhalin was an essential location for anyone wanting to really understand the whole Russian penal system. He wrote in *My Restless Life* that he relished the invitation. He wrote:

> A journey of such magnitude was not to be lightly undertaken, and the same evening found me speeding in an express train, towards the Russian capital, where I was met by Mr Galkin Vrasky. Having been assured by this gentleman that I should be furnished with even greater powers ... than on my previous journey ... I gladly undertook the task.

In early 1894, therefore, he was on his way, by sea, to Japan. From there it was a short journey across to the island of Sakhalin.

For two months, he spent time first on Sakhalin and then in Eastern Siberia. It has to be said that his picture of Sakhalin backs up that of Chekhov; here he saw the use of the 'plet' or knout – the special kind of whip used on prisoners – and he described it vividly: 'The plet ... is a terrible weapon, consisting of a lash of solid leather 3 feet long, tapering off from the handle to three circular thongs the size of a man's finger.' There was also the punishment of having a man chained to a wheelbarrow, which could be inflicted for a period of three years.

In his account of Sakhalin, Harry makes a point of being direct about his reportage: 'But I have always made it a rule to expose the dark, as well as the light, side of the Russian exile system, and can only hope that this iniquitous rule [the three-year chaining to the wheelbarrow] has been abolished.' To counterbalance this, he does depict the town of Alexandrovsky post rather cheerily: 'I have seldom visited a more attractive spot ... and as I drove from the harbour to the town, through meadows carpeted with wild flowers, some snowy peaks on the horizon, the tinkle of cattle bells, and the scent of new-mown hay, recalled summer days in Switzerland.'

Harry makes a point of doing more than simply reporting details on this trip. He made a point of going to visit one of the most notorious prisoners: Sophie Bloffstein, member of the Golden Hand radical movement. In Chekhov's book on Sakhalin, where he too met her, there is a photograph of her, standing between guards and swaddled in a long dress and a thick cloak. Chekhov saw her when she was in solitary confinement and noted that 'her hands were shackled. ... She would walk from one corner of her cell to the other, and it seemed as if she were sniffing the air the whole time, like a mouse in a trap.' On one of her many escapes there had been a murder and a robbery of a large sum. Sophie Golden Hand was a legendary figure in her time, although her life story is somewhat blurred. It seems that she died in 1902, and that she was seen by some as a figure in the Robin Hood category, never robbing the poor.

In this last trip before he spent some time at home, making ready for his next adventure in the Klondike, Harry's interest in criminology definitely matured and deepened. He made a point of seeing a prison at Nerchinsk, 'where only the most dangerous state prisoners are confined,' and then he went to Akatui Prison, which was much smaller than the usual gaol. Here he had time to note the little home comforts of the political prisoners, such as the fact that they had books and even a printing press. He commented that the governor let him spend time with these men unaccompanied, and he picked up some significant notes on them, such as the fact that one was the brother of a professor in Moscow, who was a pupil of Charcot, the famous doctor in Paris who had influenced Freud.

When Harry met Oscar Wilde in Boulogne, mentioned in my first chapter, he was, of course, one of many friends and acquaintances who had a curiosity about hard labour and life as a jailbird. Oscar was also in Andre Gide's company, for instance, and the great author of *The Importance of Being Earnest* told the young French writer that his life was always going to run its course out, and the payback would come. In other words, he was speaking frankly and off the record about his inner reflections on being imprisoned. Harry also heard these confessions, as Oscar spoke candidly with him. Wilde, with little time left to live at this point, hardly had any reason to be guarded.

The criminal interests continued. Harry took part in the 1895 Paris Prison Congress; he recalled:

> About a hundred of us sat every day at the Sorbonne to discuss various questions connected with prisoners of every class and nation. … Special attention was also devoted to crime in its medico-legal sense, and the papers of that greatest authority on the subject, Herr Kraft Ebing, afforded me keen interest.

But he was not only attending to some criminological theory: he met Monsieur Deibler, the public executioner who lived near the Gare du Nord, and the man proudly told Harry that he had in his time executed 157 persons. He offered to show Harry the guillotine, and of course, the offer was accepted.

Harry was given a guided tour, and the horrible machine was explained. Before they parted, there was this conversation:

> 'Do you ever speak with the condemned?' I asked, as we emerged into the sunlit courtyard from that shed of darkness and death. Monsieur Deibler paused and looked at me with the pale, inscrutable eyes which had placidly witnessed so many horrors.
> 'Only one word.'
> 'And that is?'
> 'Allons!'

It was now late 1895, and after a sojourn in Paris for several weeks after the Congress, Harry was restless again. What happened next was that the traveller who had been fated to become an expert on Russian prisons transmuted into a genuine explorer. He conceived the notion of shunning all comforts – with no projected steamship journeys or any time spent on trains when it came to seeing a wilderness in the world. No; he felt the attraction of undertaking a hugely challenging journey entirely by land – going from Paris to New York. That was his first idea, but it was to be aborted, and another tough challenge butted in and sent him elsewhere.

Chapter 5

Alaska and the Klondike

And now I see with eye serene
The very pulse of the machine,
A being breathing thoughtful breath,
A traveller between life and death
William Wordsworth, *She was a Phantom of Delight*

The overland trip was prompted by Lord Dunmore, travelling with Harry crossing the Channel. Dunmore, cigar in hand, said, 'I am going to try to get from New York to Paris by land!' It was probably hot air, and the aristocrat was in his cups, but the thought was planted in Harry's imagination, and there it grew.

In April 1896, Harry approached *The Pall Mall Gazette* with the idea. He reflected in *My Restless Life*, however:

For, on leaving New York, I knew no more about the regions to be traversed than when their negotiation had first been discussed on board the Channel steamer. That I must go through Alaska, cross Bering Straits, and await the winter before making my dash into unknown Asia was all I could glean at the Geographical Society in London.

His deal with *The Pall Mall* led to lots of publicity, and he soon became a celebrity, the man who was about to do something near impossible. He notes in *My Restless Life*, 'The columns of nonsense published in the New York papers about myself, were only equalled by the absurd misstatements which I constantly read on the most important questions of the day.' In fact, he was about to have a brush with death, and undergo a horrendous ordeal in the most wild and formidable climate containing human life anywhere on earth.

70

He wrote about this experience in several places, in letters as well as in his books, and spoke about it in conversation. The experience was to lead to his writing a letter to the United States government, demanding redress and punishment for the savages who had almost killed him. Perhaps the clearest and most specific account is in a report in *The Times*. Harry had set off, and had managed to get to the Bering Straits, when he fell amongst the settlement of Oumwaidjik, in the land of the Tchuktchis. *The Times* explains what that place was like:

> The Tchuktchis are wholly devoid of morality, and will barter a wife for a handful of tobacco. Infidelity is no crime among them. They number together about 5,000 and along Behring Strait are seven settlements of perhaps 300 each. … They acknowledge no government and pay no taxes. None of them had ever heard of the Tsar … There is not a tree or a blade of grass for 400 miles inland, nothing but swamp and rock. The natives die weekly of scurvy and starvation.

Later, after his second and successful expedition, he explained that as Harry and companions reached this place, their stores were taken by 'the villainous chief of the village who informed us that we were virtually his prisoners'. Harry suffered in the absolute extreme after that: 'I was attacked by scurvy and a painful skin disease, while my companion, Harding, contracted a complaint peculiar to the Tchuktchis. … But a sail appeared on the horizon.' He and Harding were rescued by Captain Joseph Whiteside, on the *Belvedere*, and a month later they were in San Francisco. He had been very fortunate. The *Belvedere* was the only vessel that would have been anywhere near that place, and all Harry had done was stick a flag in the land by the shore, praying that it would be seen. Had the ship not seen that flag, starvation would have been Harry and Harding's fate.

In *Through the Goldfields of Alaska to the Bering Straits* we have the full story of this horrendous experience. In this gruelling journey, Harry was accompanied by his manservant, George Harding, and a rugged miner called Joe Cooper, who seems to have been capable of

71

undertaking any wilderness craft or skill that might be required. They travelled from New York (firstly by rail) to Indian Point on the Bering Strait and then home again to their starting point across the North Atlantic, the latter part of the trip being the rescue after the Oumwaidjik experience. This entailed, for the first stage, a 700-mile trek to the northern end of the Chilkoot Pass, followed by another 600 miles through lakes, with portages between sailings, to Fort Selkirk (which was a ruin) and then along the vast Yukon River all the way to the coast at Michelovski (St Michael) on the Norton Sound. All this was before crossing to the ordeal of Oumwaidjik.

The last stretch, on the Yukon, may have been on a massive river – going through the Klondikes, Circle City and the huge emptiness west of Nuklukcayet (Unnlakleet), but that comparative ease was sorely needed after the first endurance test. When Harry and friends reached a peak from which they could see Lake Lindeman, where Cooper had gone on to make a rough boat for the portage stretch, Harry wrote, 'I have roughed it in most parts of the world – among others, Borneo, Siberia and Chinese Tartary – but I can safely describe that climb over the Chilkoot as the severest physical experience of my life.'

There are many reasons for the forbidding nature of the Chilkoot Pass: changeable weather, lack of food sources, deep snowdrifts, dangerous bogs, very low temperatures, and of course, the horrendous demands made on the individual's stamina and muscular strength, along with the ubiquitous plague of the mosquitoes. At this time – 1896 – Harry had not yet walked in Siberia nor experienced the tarantass mode of transport for exceptionally long distances. That was to come a few years after the Alaska trip. An instance of the difficulties involved in this section of the journey is the morass, which was reached after six hours of slogging through a rocky stretch with no path. Harry explains what happened:

In one of these bogs, where the mire was quite waist deep, a horse lost his footing and fell. More than an hour was occupied in extricating him, and indeed at one time it looked as though

he would disappear altogether, packs and all. Two swift
mountain torrents, several yards across, fed by a large glacier
this side of Chilkoot, were then forded ... the poor jaded nags
were exhausted by their struggles in the swamps, and the swift
rush of the icy cold water nearly carried them off their legs.

Harry and Harding, moving up to meet with Cooper, then met with
other travellers occasionally, including a family party on a scow, and
a lone Austrian ex-solder they called 'Dutchy'. This was nothing
compared with the string of lakes that had to be crossed, with portage,
to get the party to Fort Selkirk. Harry explained: 'The portage was
over a mile in length, and as the quantity of baggage entailed three
journeys we camped for the night near a sawmill at the head of Lake
Bennett.' What strikes the reader is the slowness and boredom this
meant; every task was a challenge to sheer labouring abilities and the
reserves of strength. On top of this, the men had to adapt and endure
when the weather was far too savage to combat, as at one point when
their tent was blown down and the party simply huddled up together
and lay by the lee of their boat in a blizzard.

   Still, in the course of this testing journey up to Fort Selkirk, there
are glimpses of answers as to why a man would undertake such a trail.
This is in the descriptive passages when Harry allows himself to do
more than simply describe or offer facts in a documentary way. For
instance, in this:

   The glorious sunshine now reveals a landscape that for the
   past three days has been shrouded in a driving mist. ... Away
   on the horizon snowy peaks 8,000 to 10,000 feet high glitter
   on every side against a cloudless blue.

Finally, after the first few thousand miles, Harry and friends arrive at
the Klondike. He had been very well informed about which areas had
been panned and dug and has a sound knowledge of the geography of
that region in which a comparatively small number of prospectors have
ventured into. In 1896, a certain George Cormack had made the first

significant discovery there; he had a store near Five Finger Rapids and had married a local Indian woman.

Harry clearly did considerable research with an eye to commercial enterprise, noting which seams and areas had been only slightly explored or tested for gold. He makes tantalizing statements that one expects would have made his readers rush out to book a passage north, such as: 'I have it on the same authority that as much as $560 was washed out of one pan at Klondike and that this marvellous gold zone extends for quite 500 miles.' Built into the descriptive passages in Harry's account of the mining fields is an explanation of how to work in extracting gold. It is almost as if he realizes that such content will help to sell the book.

As the party reached the mighty Yukon, they came to Dawson City. As he points out, this shanty (which is all it was then) was established by Joseph Ladue in September 1896. The place was named after a Dr Dawson who created the boundary between Alaska and the North-West Territory. The life there was tough, but Harry points out that the settlement had 3,000 people there before the spread of news about the gold, and that prospectors had been mistaken in thinking that Dawson City sat on top of the gold fields, which were at least 15 tough miles away.

His readers would be expecting terrible tales of suffering, of course, and Harry does include some notes on this, but in reality, it appears that the main ordeal experienced was the food shortage. Harry notes that starvation loomed as he was there, and adds that the women and children had been moved to Fort St Michael, a little further south.

In spite of the hardships, Dawson City had its diversions. On his trip north, Harry had met at one point a small travelling theatrical outfit, and now, in the town, he would note that there were two theatres, together with 'dancing saloons' and 'gambling hells'. The picture painted relates well to the popular literature of the Klondike, such as the poems of Robert Service, including *The Shooting of Dan McGrew*.

There is no denying that Harry worked into this book a great deal of travel information, aimed at those readers who were bent on doing the journey to Alaska and hoping to strike it rich. He relates sensational tales of men who had become immensely wealthy, and in addition to that, he gives detailed explanations of the routes to the gold fields. He sums up the essential information that every British reader would be wanting: 'The most direct route from England is from Liverpool to New York or Montreal, thence by Canadian Pacific Railway to Victoria BC, whence small steamers run frequently from Juneau and Skagway.'

The modern reader wonders at the hardihood of Harry and his party; most notably, perhaps, there is the question of coping with the cold. In this book on the Alaskan journey, there is little space devoted to the question: he merely mentions that when the group stopped to eat, they either cooked the fish they caught or took some of their 'trail pack' supplies of chocolate and bits of dried food. He does, however, supply a paragraph in which he tackles the subject of clothing and supplies. The guiding principle of travellers in cold climates has to be that cold and hunger go hand in hand:

> As regards outfit, do not take anything that is not absolutely necessary. ... A couple of large oilskin bags, such as sailors use, will be useful; two or three thick tweed suits, plenty of flannel underwear, six pairs of wading stockings and a good strong hunting knife ... also a couple of pairs of hair [snow] goggles.

The party then moved on, via Circle City to Fort St Michael. The names dignify them; in reality, they are collections of huts. Circle City, Harry notes, 'has been called by enthusiastic Yukoners the "Paris of Alaska",' but Harry has to disagree. Naturally, he is intrigued by the entertainment, as he always had an interest in theatre and music. He went to one shindig, and his description is summed up in few words: 'It was past midnight, but the Arctic twilight still revealed a number of mud-stained men and painted women, slowly circling round to the strains of *Donau-Wellen* [a waltz by Ivanovici] execrably played.'

As usual, Harry highlights the trials and tribulations of a place. In the case of Circle City, the dogs figure prominently: 'The Yukon dog is a terrible thief and will carry off everything from a piece of bacon to a pair of boots.' On the Lower Yukon, 'there are no places of interest.' Then, after experiencing the city, the party moves out towards St Michael, and the Alaskan part of the journey is almost over. Harry sums up the situation at that point: 'The treacherous waters of the Bering Sea are, for a wonder, smooth and sunlit, at midday, on 21 July, we anchor off Fort St Michael, the journey here from New York having occupied exactly fifty-six days.'

Across the Strait there was his terrible date of destiny, with the barbarous Tchuktchis. But there is one last and very pleasant experience before that trial of his endurance – the settlement he elected as the one place he would choose if he were forced to live in Alaska – Fort St Michael. He considered this a 'bright, clean little place' – a small island just a few miles from Alaska. The account given is of a sturdy, well cared for place compared with Circle City, and the Alaska Commercial Company was in control of the building. The photo included in the book shows a cluster of small huts, one or two towers, a church and a large hall of three floors.

Here Harry met and stayed a while with an Englishman, Mr Wilson, and he revelled in some comfort after the travails of his long journey. He was 'soon installed in a pretty bedroom with chintz curtains under the agent's hospitable roof, wondering whether this were not all a dream.' He even enjoyed whisky and cigars; but this place was, as he put it, 'the last port generally visited by Arctic expeditions before entering the frozen region'.

The last phase of *Through the Goldfields of Alaska to the Bering Straits* is an enthralling narrative of the de Windt party in the hands of the chief, Koari, and the Tchuktchi tribe at Oumwaidjik. The situation escalates into one of extreme fear, as Harry perceives that the supposed guides and appointed local experts are in fact stealing from him, bullying him, and planning to hold the three men as prisoners. This is in a society that practises any number of amoral acts as they are devoid of any morality that relates to European values, principally in the cultural tradition of 'kamitok', which is the ritual killing of elders, with the willing co-operation of the victims, when the time has come (by common agreement) for the aged one to die. But on top of this, the tribe is described as being capable of eating anything that moves, and of killing anything that moves when in their cups.

By early October things were looking very bleak. Harry writes, 'The daylight was fast leaving us. … We had until this time kept a bright lookout for the Andrée Polar Balloon, which we should have greeted with open arms.' Matters reached the depths of fear and apprehension one day when the Tchuktchis, being drunk, had fired guns, and one man had fired a Winchester rifle at Koari's head – fortunately missing the target.

Harry, pushed to the limits of his patience, as he was anxious to arrange a dog sled and push in into Eastern Siberia, described a confrontation with the chief, which led to this: 'I could have struck the scoundrel in the face as the nameless horrors of an imprisonment in filth and darkness for seven or eight endless months were revealed in all their hideous reality.' This was the point at which the party saw the truth of their situation: they would probably die of starvation in that long winter if they could not be rescued, and very soon. Enter the *Belvedere*, in the nick of time. Harry notes, as he and the party stood at the edge of land and watched their saviour negotiate the icy bay, 'Koari never left us for an instant. "You no go," he kept repeating, "big water, you drown." This looked extremely likely. We were indeed between the devil and the deep blue sea.'

But the steam whaler, *Belvedere*, came to them; it was on its way back south to San Francisco after two years in the Arctic. The sense of freedom was an elation that Harry, Harding and Cooper had not known before. The only fear now was the weather: they had to endure a savage gale *en route* for civilization. But Harry, as he so often does, explains away any ordeal by making it relative to something else: 'I have often felt more anxiety on board a gigantic liner in a moderate gale than during the dirtiest weather on the tight, trim little *Belvedere*.'

He was soon in San Francisco, but there was a recuperation period desperately needed. He had contracted a skin disease, and was in a very low condition. He recalls that when he boarded the vessel *Bear*, which he knew from the past, he was hardly recognized by those who knew him. He wrote, 'This is, perhaps, scarcely surprising, for a glance in the mirror reflects a countenance that would do credit to the filthiest and most debased Tchuktchi.'

In *My Restless Life*, Harry comments on his situation at that point in life, about 1897: 'Although I did not receive any monetary advantage from the Alaskan gold strike itself, I certainly benefited by it indirectly, for my book on the journey to the Bering Straits had an enormous sale, being published simultaneously in London and New York.' He adds that it was bought as a guide book rather than a work with 'literary merit'. But here he is too modest. True, the book has a thread of instruction and advice, aiming to be a *vade mecum* for any traveller following Harry's itinerary; but it has a high level of wonderfully expressive description, often with a poetic vocabulary that heightens it into far more that a factual guide.

At this point, Harry found time to marry for the second time, and he writes in *My Restless Life* that had it not been for his new wife, Hilda, he would never have succeeded in what was coming up as the next and greatest venture – the trip from Paris to New York by land. He explains, 'Some say that explorers have no right to marry but my case proves to be at least one exception to this rule.' We have to recall here that his first marriage had failed and the divorce granted for 'desertion'. It would not be unfair to say that Harry never really appeared to place anything concerning emotions and allegiances above the burning desire to struggle onwards in wild, barren places. The newly married man was eager for more financial security, and he did try to form a syndicate to finance a business venture in the Klondike, but it failed. He explained, with palpable regret, 'Let me clearly state that I do not, for one moment, blame the Chairman or Board of my company for the disaster. I simply regard the whole thing as bad luck.' And he states, 'What the public lost, for the sake of £30,000, may now be calculated by the fact that three of the claims of which I held the option afterwards realized over two millions sterling.'

The enterprise had been a bold one, well backed; a prospectus was issued, and *The Times* carried a detailed version of this on 14 February 1898, with the heading 'The "De Windt" Exploration Company (Limited)'. Harry had managed to acquire the services of well established and highly esteemed professionals for this plan: his bankers were the Union Bank of London; his accountants were Price, Waterhouse; and his consulting engineers were the Shelfords of Westminster, respected members of the Institute of Civil Engineering. The aim was clear and direct: 'Mr de Windt proposes to start again for Alaska in conjunction with mining engineers and a competent staff at the earliest possible opportunity. His arrangements in this respect have been long matured, and are full and complete.' Here we have a glimpse of the Harry de Windt who would have done very well today, as an entrepreneur; he knew how to 'brand' himself. When it came to 'puff', he was neat and impressive: 'Mr de Windt is well known to the public as one of the first explorers to go through the Klondike gold-bearing district and Alaska.'

It must have been a profound disappointment to him when the master plan failed. He had even recruited the Earl of Lonsdale as a director. It must have looked like a viable plan, but the takers were too few.

This failure is indeed surprising, as, within six months of July 1897, when the steamer *Portland* docked at Seattle with a ton of gold on board, 100,000 prospectors started the journey to the gold fields. All this had stemmed from a discovery made in Rabbit Creek in August 1896 at the Yukon, when three men found gold – one of them with the interesting name of Skookum Jim Mason.

In reality, up in the wild Klondike Harry described so invitingly, the madness was in full swing. Pierre Berton, author of one of the standard works on the Klondike, describes this powerfully:

> All winter long, sourdoughs and cheechakos [tourists] alike were haunted by the idea that all the gold had not yet been uncovered in the Klondike area. Scarcely a month passed without a stampede into the hills as whispers of secret finds filtered across the camp. ... An old man in a cabin on the Yukon reported gold on Rosebud Creek, 50 miles above Dawson, and every man who could make the journey rushed to it in the dark of the night.

Harry the writer did not waste any time in building on his reputation as a writer as well as a traveller. He published *True Tales of Travel and Adventure*, and he was now living in Paris, back to his roots. In fact, he had been busy writing for periodicals in between visits to French race meetings, and as always, he was a restless spirit with a profound need to be in society and to cultivate friendships. In his autobiographical writings, Harry says practically nothing about that quality in him that led to *True Tales of Travel and Adventure*. The book has a great deal to recommend it, and should not be passed over as a mere collection of trifles – pieces that would fill up a volume. Arguably, the book has some unknown gems of adventure writing, and these show the strand in Harry's creativity that should perhaps have been given more light of day had he not continued the treks across the globe.

The collection is a mix of pieces that develop his travel experiences (such as a factual documentary feature on whaling), short impressionistic essays, and first-person accounts of criminological encounters. On top of this there are a few short exercises in pure fiction. The book is undoubtedly a collection that maximizes the writing from notebooks as he moved around the world from the 1870s onwards, but in some of these we may see the writer who was at the time progressing into journalistic work for the growing periodical market. The 1890s was the time when new literary journals mushroomed, catering partly for the male readership who had so enthusiastically engaged with the male romance of writers such as H. Rider Haggard and Robert Louis Stevenson. The literary journals were a lively mixture of serialized fiction, complete stories, documentary, and first-person narratives. *The Strand Magazine* (1891) had been one of the first of this new breed, followed by *The Idler* (1892) and then *Pearson's Magazine* (1896). This changing face of reading for the more lowbrow literary tastes matched the new humour too, as exemplified in Jerome K. Jerome's *Three Men in a Boat* (1889) and George and Weedon Grossmith's *Diary of a Nobody* (1892). The readers of the 1890s wanted adventure, information and a type of humour that did not depend on being deeply well read in the classics or very learned about history and art. Sport was a popular subject, along with travel and hobbies.

This burgeoning market was ideal for the newly married Harry de Windt, with his wife and responsibilities, of course; but he was financially very well off at this time. As usual with him, writing was of course a means to earn money, but he was a compulsive writer. His book *My Notebook at Home and Abroad* gives ample evidence of the fact that he had a massive resource of 'material' for a very wide range of writing across several genres. At the opening of that book, he wrote, 'Thirty odd notebooks lie before me; milestones marking the progress of what, I suppose, may be termed a fairly eventful life. Each tattered cover bears a label indicating where its contents were scrawled amid surroundings ranging from an Imperial palace to a tiny canvas tent.' As compulsive writers know well, there is no such thing as boredom, if one is able to write anywhere and any time. Harry clearly had that faculty.

Chapter 6

From Paris to New York by Land

The coldest temperature ever recorded on the Earth is -89 degrees C (-129° F) and was measured at a Russian research station at Vostok on the Antarctic ice cap.

Frances Ashcroft, *Life at the Extreme*

Harry wasted no time in capitalizing on his new experience. When his health was restored, he was busy again. On 16 April 1897, *The Times* announced that he was 'shortly to leave England on a lecturing tour in the United States.' He had come to know some parts of the States before the journey to Alaska, and he wrote in *My Restless Life* a short account of his stay in New York at that time. He met the poet Ella Wheeler Wilcox and Richard Mansfield, the tragic actor; but overall he was not impressed by the city. He reflected that, even being a guest at the famous Waldorf hotel, he 'could not get a decent meal in the place.' Harry was a Parisian, it should be remembered; although he constantly refers to himself as an Englishman, it is to Paris that he refers when in need of a touchstone of civilized society and the good life as he saw it.

He was also displeased with the American press, writing that there were 'columns of nonsense' about him in the daily papers. But he did take up lecturing, and did very well. He worked in England as well, talking about the Klondike. In February 1898, for instance, he spoke at the Imperial Institute. At that lecture, he had to do what he did so many times – dispel rumours and hyperbolic writing about the frozen wastes, but it is clear that he injected some humour. *The Times* correspondent wrote: 'Mrs Berry, who was married at Klondike, lifted ten thousand pounds sterling from her husband's claim in her spare moments (laughter).'

He did lecture in the States, though, for two consecutive winters, and he explains in *My Notebook at Home and Abroad* that the lecture tour was organized by Major Pond, 'that renowned impresario'. This was James Burton Pond, who had been born in Allegany County, New York, in 1838 and had grown up in Wisconsin. He became a fighter with the Third Wisconsin Cavalry in 1859 and served as a captain in the Civil War. It was in the eighties that he became a lecture manager. Pond was a man after Harry's own heart: he had run away from home and followed a life of variety and adventure. He also had a career as a writer and journalist, editing a provincial paper in Wisconsin, and then, in relation to working with his most famous lecturer, Mark Twain, he wrote a journal account of the journey he had accomplished just before booking Harry – a trip with Twain on a world tour. Clearly, Pond was a PR man and took charge of Twain's publicity.

Harry toured in New York, Philadelphia and Boston, and again, he was not impressed. He wrote that the 'social leaders further West occasionally displayed a rather disconcerting lack of civility and refinement.' His tour included some farcical and fascinating experiences. One time he was mistaken for a 'humble showman' and was asked to wait in the servants' quarters, but there he met a Mr Stokes who turned out to be wonderful company, and the night was made memorable. In Washington, he lectured before President Theodore Roosevelt, and again, the occasion turned from seriousness to farce. The master of ceremonies for the evening was the explorer Admiral Peary, and he kept forgetting that he was supposed to introduce Harry, who sat patiently waiting for his introduction. It never came, and only when Peary left the platform did he suddenly recall that there was a guest speaker. Peary then said, 'Oh, here is Harry de Windt. … He has just come here by land from Paris!' He also met Alexander Graham Bell, and several Mormons – everything presenting him with amusing experiences.

But it was Roosevelt who left him with the most remarkable memory. He was treated to a very English meal at the White House, and he relished the atmosphere of 'cheerfulness and lack of ceremony'. Roosevelt, he noted, 'had all the grace and energy of a lad of twenty' and indeed the President was well briefed: 'I was most impressed by my host's marvellously accurate knowledge of Arctic Alaska.'

Naturally, they spoke of Siberia, as everyone in Harry's company did. The question of the great northern wastes being crossed by rail intrigued Roosevelt the traveller and man's man. Roosevelt requested that Harry must 'place a car at his disposal on the first Paris-bound express, but the moment after had dropped all levity, and warmly shaking my hand, said some kind things anent … our "great journey" and its accomplishment.'

Then, in the summer of 1901, it was time for Harry to set about a return to Siberia – and, in fact, to travel by land, starting from Paris, and trek from there to New York. This was to be the feat for which he was most celebrated and remembered. His book on this journey was to become his most highly rated work, and was later reprinted in popular library editions, notably in the Nelson Shilling Library, alongside such luminaries as the English judge, Lord Brampton, the poet Robert Browning, and G.W. Steevens, who produced the great work *With Kitchener to Khartoum*, on Victoria's most celebrated hero.

In September 1901, not long before departure, the press announced the expedition, the key statement being, 'Now … the explorer is receiving help from the Russian and American authorities … Mr de Windt's chief objective is to survey the country to the north-east of Yakutsk, to which point the Russian government and a Franco-American syndicate are projecting a railway from Irkutsk.'

What Harry referred to as 'the de Windt expedition' consisted of himself, his faithful servant George Harding and the Vicomte de Clinchamp – the latter 'a young Frenchman who acted as photographer'. They gathered in Paris and Harry sorted out the necessary provisions. Before setting off by train to Moscow for the first leg, Harry finalized provisions, but in *From Paris to New York by Land* he explained, 'Suffice it to say that, although the minutest care and attention were lavished on the organization of our food supply, lack of transport in the Far North compelled me to abandon most of our provisions … more than once we were in measurable distance from starvation.'

A photo of the three adventurers adorns *My Restless Life*, showing a very different scene than the little party in the buffet of the Gare du

Nord where 'a stirrup-cup was insisted upon by some of de Clinchamp's enthusiastic compatriots.' It shows the three men totally enveloped in rich, solid fur trappings: they have thick, high boots, massive gloves, knee-length overcoats and hoods that cover all but the very front of their faces, and the latter are swaddled in the bushy beards and moustaches in the case of Harding and de Clinchamp. As for Harry, he has his moustache only. The note to the photo encapsulates the achievement: 'The first successful overland expedition Paris–New York, 1901–1902.'

The itinerary they planned was to go by train to Moscow, then to move on to Irkutsk. From there a sleigh was used to follow the route of the Lena post road as far as Yakutsk; after that it was into the wilder stretches of Siberia to the Bering Strait, across to Alaska and then down south to New York. The last stretch in the United States was by rail again. The first railroad run presented only the problem of boredom, as the scenery was all the same – endless tracts of open land with occasional forests. Irkutsk, fortunately, found them with some good fortune, as the local Chief of Police was helpful and made sure that they had suitably sturdy sleighs.

These rough vehicles, staple transport in Siberia, are vividly described as Harry guides the reader through the preparations for the tough middle passage of the epic journey:

> A Yakute sleigh has a pair of runners, but otherwise totally differs from any other sleigh in the wide world. Imagine a sack of coarse matting about 4 feet deep suspended from a frame of rough wooden poles in a horizontal triangle, which also forms a seat for the driver. Into this bag the traveller first lowers his luggage, then his mattress, pillows and furs, and finally enters himself, lying at full length upon his belongings.

Such was the conveyance used by the intrepid explorers. The main enemy – frostbite – was supposedly shielded away by a flap that covered the face. But all this was very little protection. They were setting off in winter (for reasons to do with the dangers of wet and boggy land at the Bering Strait end of the land tract), and in Siberia, temperatures drop to below -60° C in winter. Harry always had but a vague idea about the dangers of cold. He knew that the basic principle of dressing as the natives dress was one to be followed, and that food was essential, and in large quantities. But other than that, he took risks, as his knowledge was limited, and in that he was no different from the travellers before him. We now know, for instance, that Sir Ranulph Fiennes's trek across Antarctica on foot meant that he and his partner, Dr Mike Stroud, ideally needed 6,500 calories a day. But with current physiological knowledge, they could adapt and 'cut corners' regarding the weight they carried and their amount of food intake. In her book *Life at the Extremes*, Frances Ashcroft discusses this, and adds, 'By the time they reached the South Pole they were emaciated, sick, very hungry, and had each lost more than 20 kilos. … Stroud calculated that on one day he had used an astonishing 11,650 calories, the highest expenditure ever recorded in man.' Harry and party would have been in a similar situation had they not used the sleighs, of course. It might have been dangerous in the Yakute sleigh in terms of extreme cold and frostbite, but at least they were using very few calories.

Harry, as an expert on prisons and therefore well informed regarding the closely calculated dietaries that had been introduced into the British penal system after 1877, would have been aware of the need for sufficient food to be eaten to match the degree of physical labour a man undertakes, but this was very approximate and involved questionable guesswork when the basic principle was shifted from convict labour in Dartmoor to slogging through blizzards in Siberia. His remedy in effect was to make sure that small amounts of food were taken little and often.

Back home, his wife of just two years, Hilda, was surely well aware of her husband's tendency to disappear for long periods. She was the youngest daughter of the Reverend William Robinson Clark, who was at one time Vicar of Taunton. Hilda was to experience another twenty-three years of Harry and his wanderlust, although fortunately, apart from a jaunt to the Balkans, this Siberian adventure was to be his last long-distance trek. Unlike his first wife, Hilda was to see plenty of her husband in the Edwardian and Great War years, although he was always an incessant adventurer: if it wasn't Irkutsk it was Cornwall, or Paris or North Africa. Married or single, he chased the dream and found it hard to sit still. Perhaps Hilda was that typical long-suffering Victorian wife/daughter, inured to life with ambitious males who were either promoting the Christian life or pushing the boundaries of commerce and empire, leaving the womenfolk to care for the home. But of course, there were plenty of female Victorian travellers; the issue as to whether or not Hilda would ever travel with Harry was surely never raised for debate.

By the last years of the nineteenth century, the Russian Empire had expanded into a number of 'fronts'. Secure frontiers were needed, hence the long machinations of the Great Game of espionage between the forces of Russia and Britain. By 1858 there was the maritime province, which was the long coast opposite Sakhalin Island; then there was the border with the Chinese Empire, from which Manchuria was to be occupied in 1900, while Harry was over in the United States; finally, there was the Southern front, which was partly formed by the border with Korea. Little did Harry realize, as he travelled the length of Siberia, that major wars involving Russia were looming in the near future.

Over the previous centuries, the indigenous peoples of Siberia had gradually settled in three discernible bands across the vast continent: the Yakuts to the north; the Tunguses to the south, and, furthest east, the Koriaks. Harry, in *From Paris to New York by Land* is always interested in the ethnography, history and cultural traditions of these people and of any other tribal settlements within the land crossing his route. As he set out from Irkutsk, for instance, he follows the Lena post road, and there, still 1,500 miles from the Sea of Okhotsk and a further thousand north of that to the Bering Strait, he makes a point of dwelling on the Skoptsi. He was well aware that there had been media interest in this sect back home in the West, as these people were viewed as being morally revolting by the Christian British and other Europeans, the main reason for this being the Skopsti practice of castration. Their name is Russian for 'castrated'. They also believed in the necessity of female mastectomy, related to the teachings that were strongly against sexual desire and fornication. The basis of these beliefs was that, after the Fall from Eden, halves of the forbidden fruit were grafted on to the bodies of Adam and Eve, and these formed testicles and breasts. The whole sect began in the eighteenth century, with a leader called Selivanov.

Only twenty years before Harry's visit in which he met them and stayed with some, there had been repressive measures against the Skoptsi; many were deported and a large number ran westwards to Romania. Harry, in line with the typical Victorian traveller, stays safety in the realms of generality when he describes them:

> Most of the men are enormously stout, with smooth flabby faces and dull heavy eyes, while the women have an emaciated and prematurely old appearance. The creed is no doubt a revolting one, physically and morally, but with all the faults, the Skopt has certain good points which his free neighbours in Yakutsk might do well to imitate.

The Skopts were in exile at that time. Harry could not help but be impressed by their order and cleanliness when he commented on their settlement, Markha: 'The scrupulous cleanliness of Markha after the dirt and squalor of most Siberian villages was striking.' He was impressed that the houses of the Skopts had books and newspapers in evidence, and that they produced enough food for subsistence.

The party carried on to Yakutsk and there they met the usual problems of delay and doubletalk. Harry did what he always did when in trouble – he employed a local. In this case it was a Cossack called Stepan Rastorguyeff, who was to be their guide for the next long stretch, following the river Lena, which runs north to the shores of the Arctic Ocean. The greatest obstacle at this point, by Yakutsk, was a combination of seasonal bad weather and an epidemic. He was aiming to reach Sredni-Kolymsk in the north, and he heard news that this little place was in the grip of a famine. The outlook was grim. Yet, there was help; the officials were mostly co-operative and practical. The

A picture of Harry in his English gentleman's attire. (*My Restless Life*)

Sir Charles Brooke (1829–1917), Second Rajah of Sarawak (1868–1916). Charles married Harry's sister, Margaret, in 1869, and gave Harry his first taste of Eastern adventure. (Wellcome Images/ Wikimedia)

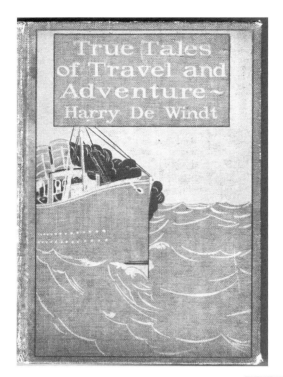

Harry de Windt's *True Tales of Travel and Adventure*, 1899. (Author's collection)

A letter, dated 12 December 1900, from Harry to the painter Caton Woodville, written in his club, the Junior United Service Club, in Pall Mall.

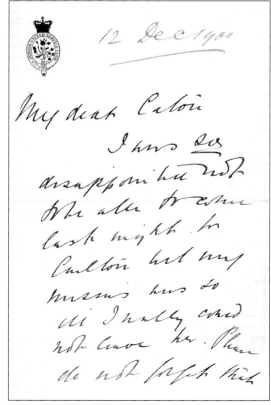

A Bosnian smuggler – a typical
portrait from Harry's European
adventure.
(*Through Savage Europe*)

Cape Despair – one
of the most desolote
locations of the
Siberian trip.
(*From Paris to New
York by Land*)

An illustration depicting part of the ride to India across Persia and Baluchistan. This was one of Harry's more uncomplicated journeys. The route and notes suggest that he was playing a part in the spying activities of the 'Great Game'. (*A Ride to India across Persia and Baluchistan*)

The Palace of the Khan at Kelát, Baluchistan, a city constructed as a huge oblong, and a very sound position for defence in times of trouble. Harry would have known that this destination was familiar to the military intelligence officers of the army.
(*A Ride to India across Persia and Baluchistan*)

A view of Tiflis (today this is Tbilisi). In Harry's day it was a distant administrative region of the Russian Empire. (*A Ride to India across Persia and Baluchistan*)

On the long journey to either *katorga* or to a prison settlement, barges such as this were used where there was a stretch of river. (*Siberia As It Is*)

The tarantass was Harry's mode of transport in one phase of the Russian trek. He would have seen very little of the passing scenery. (*From Pekin to Calais by Land*)

Some local Eskimo girls, met on the Siberian journey. (*From Paris to New York by Land*)

Harry and friends, left to right: the Vicomte de Clinchamp, Harry de Windt, and George Harding. The original caption declares this as the first successful overland expedition Paris–New York, 1901–1902. (*My Restless Life*)

Harry in his full Alaskan attire. (*From Paris to New York by Land*)

The Ranee of Sarawak, Harry's
sister Margaret, who married Rajah
Charles Brooke.
(*My Life in Sarawak*, Margaret
Brooke, Ranee of Sarawak, 1913)

The interior of the Astana, the palace in Kuching,
Sarawak, built by Rajah Brook, as a wedding gift
to his wife.
(*My Life in Sarawak*, Margaret Brooke, Ranee of
Sarawak, 1913)

The town of Plevna, scene of the battle in the Russo-Turkish War. (*Through Savage Europe*)

One of Melton Prior's more dramatic drawings, showing Sir George Colley at Majuba Hill in the Transvaal War, published in *The Illustrated London News* on 14 May 1881. Harry knew Prior, who was one of many seasoned travellers he got to know when socializing in his literary clubs. (Library of Congress)

King Peter I of Serbia, the last king of that state. He was one of several dignitaries Harry met on his Balkan travels.
(Library of Congress)

Isabelle Eberhardt was a writer and traveller, best known for her writing about the desert nomads. Harry met her in Algeria on his North African visit.
(Wikimedia Commons)

A drawing of a Tchuktchi walrus hunt in the Bering Strait. (*Through the Gold-Fields of Alaska to the Bering Straits*)

A Tchuktchi home, made of walrus hide. Harry and party stayed in a large version of this. (*Through the Gold-Fields of Alaska to the Bering Straits*)

Charley, one of the tribal chiefs encountered in the Arctic. (*Through the Gold-Fields of Alaska to the Bering Straits*)

A drawing of King's Island, on the remote Bering Sea. (*Through the Gold-Fields of Alaska to the Bering Straits*)

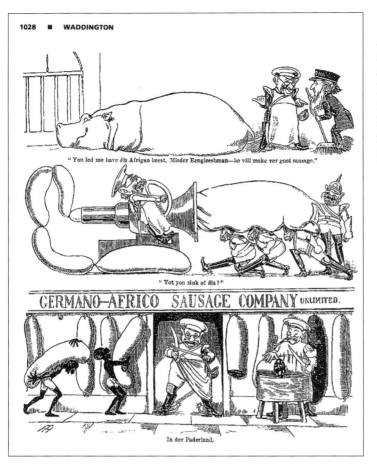

An anti-German advert. When Harry commanded the POW camp, it was in this atmosphere of hatred and spy mania.
(Author's collection)

A cartoon from the 12 July 1919 issue of *John Bull* magazine commenting on one of Horatio Bottomley's fundraising scams. He specialized in apparently patriotic schemes, but these actually put money in his own pocket.
(Wikimedia Commons)

Arthur Orton was the unsuccessful Tichborne Claimant, whose trial kept the lawyers busy for over a year. He was visited in prison and later in lodgings by Harry, and by Harry's Crimes Club friend, Churton Collins.
(Boston Medical Library/Wikimedia)

The library of the Athenaeum Club, c. 1900.
(Author's collection)

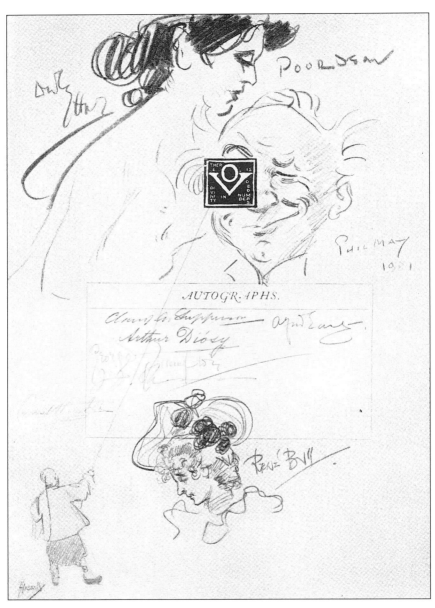

A menu from a literary club, with signatures of celebrities. (*Sixty Years Ago and After*, Max Pemberton 1936)

next stage involved travel on a *narta* rather than sleighs. This was a reindeer sled, and Harry saw this as mainly an improvement in comfort, although, as he put it, 'over rough ground their very lightness makes them roll and pitch about like a cross-Channel steamer.'

Still, provisions were gathered, and they had Stepan to give advice. They took black bread, salt fish, tinned food, and, as Harry puts it, 'a portion of some animal unknown'. This was almost certainly horsemeat – a delicacy in those parts. Six *nartas* set off for the north, after a dinner party and many warm farewells. Harry notes the situation then: 'An hour later the lights of Yakutsk had faded away on the horizon, and we had bidden farewell to civilization which was only regained six long months later, at the gold-mining city of Nome in Alaska.'

They were now depending on the compass and the stars to take them to their next posting house. There was a choice of routes, and none of these could be accurately described as roads. Travel now depended on the post houses, and these were mostly dreadful, but on the Lena run, some were just about tolerable. Harry often describes these places in his books on Siberia, usually delineating the horrors of stench and grime. Of course, he lived at a time when the transference of disease was still little known. Had he known about fleas and lice, and their part in such diseases as typhus and plague, he would have perhaps thought twice about this kind of experience at a post house:

At first we suffered severely from nausea in these unsavoury shelters, and there were other reasons for this which cannot here be explained. Suffice it to say that it was a constant source of wonder to me that even this degraded race of beings could live amidst such bestial surroundings and yet survive. Vermin had up till now been a trifling inconvenience, but thousands on the Lena were here succeeded by myriads of the foe … our health suffered from the incessant irritation, which caused us many days of misery and nights of unrest.

The resting places were either *povarnias* (mud huts) or *stancias* ('dark,

uninhabited hovels') and often there was a trek lasting nine or ten
hours between each one of these. Time and time again, Harry is
disgusted by the conditions of the resting places; when his party
reached Verkhoyansk, it was with great relief. This town was, in 1900,
known as the 'heart of Siberia'. In fact, it was a gathering of about
fifty mud-plastered log huts in poor repair.

The party relied for help and information at each place along the
route on the local *izpravnik*. The nearest European equivalent to this
official appears to be a mix of mayor and foreman. In the little
community of about 400 people, he was responsible for security and
survival, and Harry had his letter of introduction from the Moscow
governor, so he had help from the various *izpravniki* along the
itinerary. The locals were a mix of Yakutes, exiles and settlers, and so
Harry, as he always did, met some of the political exiles. Meeting these
types would always bring a little more enlightenment regarding Russia
at the time, and Harry, for reasons he would make clear in his book,
Russia as I Know It, this was becoming his special area of expertise.
In this case he met a couple called Abramovitch, who were almost at
the point of being given their freedom.

Always aware of the need for accuracy and documentary
authenticity after the confrontation with those who insisted on Siberia
being a total hell for exiles and prisoners, Harry makes sure in this
instance that he supplies some details:

> I closely questioned Abramovitch as to the conditions of life
> at Verkhoyansk and he said that so far as the treatment of the
> exiles was concerned there was nothing to complain of, but
> the miserable pittance allowed by the government for the
> lodging and maintenance of each exile was, he justly averred,
> totally inadequate. ... My friend was therefore reduced to the
> dim light shed by his flickering logs of his fire throughout the
> dreary winter, when daylight disappears for two months.

Harry, on the whole, is cheery and stoical in the Arctic regions. He
wrote: 'I can assure the reader that I have suffered more from cold in

Piccadilly on a damp, chilly November day than in the coldest weather in this part of Siberia.' That seems a little too optimistic. He needed his stoicism. The stay at Verkhoyansk was riddled with problems. He had almost 2,000 miles between his party and the Bering Strait, and now here he was, being harassed by the local chief of police, who kept insisting that the journey be abandoned. But no, after suffering the man's pressures and laments about the tract of land ahead, Harry and friends set off into what in his book he calls 'darkest Siberia'. Here he was to be severely tested.

The next stage of the journey took the party to arguably the most depressing and neglected location in all Siberia as Harry saw it. This was Sredni-Kolymsk, which made Harry think of the great Italian poet, Dante, and his depiction of Hell, referring to the outpost of empire as 'Arctic Inferno'. Reading Harry's account here, the reader needs to think of the condition of Russia in about 1900, particularly with the growth of aggressive radicalism in mind. The serfs had been liberated in 1861 and the provincial centres of Western Russia were open to reform to a certain degree, as intellectuals published widely and feverishly in an atmosphere of increasing modernity. Although the Tsar still reigned supreme, there was action as well as talk, in the last decades of the century, with a turning point in the whole government of Russia being arrived at when Tsar Alexander II was murdered at St Petersburg in 1881, after several other attempts on his life.

The background to this kind of desperate political act was the prominence of hard-line activists who wanted revolution in Russia – a nation without a Romanov tsar. This was to happen in 1917, of course, when the Russian Revolution actually did happen and Tsar Nicholas II and his family were murdered at Yekaterinburg. Harry was in Siberia a mere seventeen years before that, and only five years before the failed revolution of 1905. It therefore comes as no surprise to learn that Harry was particularly interested not only in the penal system, but in the political exiles and the reasons why they were outcast in these rotting colonies thousands of miles from European Russia.

It is evident from Harry's assessment of Sredni-Kolymsk, where he met a group of writers and thinkers who were seen as outstandingly threatening to the Tsarist regime, that he is keen to make clear his stance on explaining the exile and prison system to his British readers. In fact, in this context, he does convey a far more critical summary of the exiles and their melancholy lives.

Sredni-Kolymsk he saw as 'an encampment deserted by trappers, or some village decimated by some deadly sickness: anything but the abode of human beings'. He called it 'the most gloomy, God-forsaken spot on this earth'. Not long before the party arrived, the chief of police had been murdered, there were suicides fairly regularly, and worst of all was the horrendous mix of disease and starvation that prevailed. The inhabitants – a mere 400 – suffered all this, but there was something else he picked up on, and that was evidence of a concept that had been built into the exile system. In Russian this was known as *bolshaya zone*, and this translates as 'the big prison zone'. Basically, this refers to the element in distant and paralysed exile beyond any actual wall or wire. Harry made this a major part of his report on the place: 'The most pitiable characteristic about Sredni-Kolymsk is the morbid influence of the place and its surroundings on the mental powers.' He goes on to explain, 'The first thing noticeable about those who had passed some years here was the utter vacancy of mind, even of men who in Europe had shone in the various professions.' He met a Polish author (whose name was kept out of the account) and this man gave a profound explanation, from his heart:

'That,' he said, '... silence ... day after day, year after year, not a sound. I have stood in that street at mid-day and heard a watch tick in my pocket. Think of it, Mr de Windt. I myself arrived here only a few months ago, but even I shall soon have to get away for a change or ...' and he tapped his forehead significantly.

Harry also met and learned from, at first hand, some notorious anarchists, such as 'Madame Akimova, who was found with explosives concealed about her person at the coronation of Nicholas

II'. Although he says little about her here, in *Russia as I Knew It* Harry gives an explanation of her crime:

> Akimova was well-born and still young in years, spoke several languages fluently and had taken high honours at the Paris Conservatoire of Music. And I learned, from this wretched exile's own lips, how her plans had been thwarted only just in time by the secret police, and how she had nearly succeeded in killing the now ex-Emperor.

The summing-up that Harry provides regarding the penal system reads like an apologia for his earlier statements in which he perhaps overstated the case in favour of humane treatment; he wrote, in concluding his chapter on this place of deprivation and comfortless solitude, in response to one exile's request of 'You will tell them in England of our life.' The sentence in question perhaps gives some support to Kennan's charges: 'For the first time in thirty years I am able to give an unofficial account of the life of these unfortunates, and to deliver to the world their piteous appeal for deliverance.' He had seen the truth about the *bolshaya zone*. It was undoubtedly a subtle and calculated notion – to imprison by means of an open sky and a vast region of bog land and ice mountain. The Tsarist administrators had conceived of a life of exile that, in many ways, was worse than close incarceration and a diet of gruel.

The next stage was by dog sled, which would take the party to the land of the Tchuktchis, and surely the very word for these people would have sent a shiver down Harry's spine, given his terrible experience at their hands a few years previously. Stepan managed to buy enough dogs for several teams and reserves for the arduous journey that lay ahead, and they were soon moving along the Lower Kolyma River. In early 1900, they reached Nijni-Kolymsk, and there was little there any better than the last place. The lesson had been learned that short stays were preferable, as the small, desperate communities along the Arctic found it almost impossible to stir and apply work and organization in any sphere. Harry notes, with a mood of determination, that the drivers refused to carry on, being scared of the next run across to the Tchuktchis, and he adds, with their spokesman, Mikouline in mind, that plying him with vodka was the best plan. It worked. The team pressed on to the really formidable, vegetation-free land where the *poorga*, or Arctic typhoon, was close by. From then on, as far as the end of the Kolyma, it was to be a case of meeting tiny settlements or dour individuals who were somehow scraping a living, with very few resources. Harry was now truly in wild territory, and although he had some knowledge of the works of previous explorers in that area, there was little he could rely on. He does, however, mention that one map-maker, Schalarof, had provided a helpful and accurate chart.

The weather was extremely changeable, and after a stretch of mild weather, 'a shrieking *poorga*' came along, and as Harry notes, that forced them to encamp. In this slow progress, with all strength and resolution tested to the extreme, the food supply was crucially important, and Harry mentions that he had taken a special food he called Carnyl, which was eaten with frozen fish. It appears to have been his saviour, whatever it was. Most likely it was a high protein food, and he mentions that one of his many professional friends had provided it for the expedition.

Once again, here he was, in the land of the Tchuktchi. He must have had nightmares simply contemplating his arrival there as he battled through the storms and ice. Near the end of that section of his journey before the coastal areas, he had also had to cope with the unseen as well as the visible obstructions to progress – in this case, ghosts. This was at Bassarika, a place in which all the inhabitants had recently died, mainly from smallpox. The drivers reckoned that it was 'an abiding-place of evil spirits'. Once again, Harry found himself placating his chief guide, Mikouline, who was a thorn in the flesh for the whole extent of this trip to the coast and the Strait. But the shadowy figure of George Harding emerges rather more substantially in the narrative here, as it was Harry's birthday (9 April) and George Harding miraculously produced a plum pudding for the occasion. But the party pushed on, keeping aside their store of booze, ready to give to the

Tchuktchis, to stem trouble. Then, within a short drive from Cape Shelagskoi and the Tchuktchis, Harry's party reached arguably the nadir of their expedition. Harry explains the situation with his usual melancholy:

> everything went wrong. ... First it was the dogs, as famished as ourselves, who dragged their tired limbs more and more heavily ... every morning I used to look at their gaunt flanks and hungry eyes. ... Then the Russian drivers, secretly backed by Mikouline, threatened almost daily to desert us. ... Only ten days out from Kolyma we were living on a quarter of a pound of Carnyl and a little frozen fish a day, a diet that would scarcely satisfy a healthy child.

Tea and tobacco kept their spirits up, and morale was just maintained. But on top of all this, one dog contracted rabies and had to be shot. It was truly the lowest and most dispiriting episode in this epic trek. Harry makes a point of praising his companions as this juncture, and rightly so: 'And I may add no leader of an expedition could wish for three more courageous comrades than the Vicomte de Clinchamp, George Harding, and last but not least, Stepan Rastorguyeff.'

Nine men and sixty ravenous dogs forced their way on fuelled by fish and Carnyl; and then, as it was thought that a Tchuktchi village was reached, it proved to be a mirage, or rather, a desolate spot where one that *had* been such a village, but it was no more. One last blizzard assailed them before they emerged at Cape Shelagskoi and to a settlement – 'two or three woebegone creatures in ragged deerskins' crawled out to greet them.

Harry, of course, already burned by his earlier contact with the Tchuktchis, was well aware of what would happen should he make a mistake in his relations with them this time. The first experience on arrival was hardly reassuring though – a group of corpses was evident, simply lying on the ground where they had perished of starvation. Harry and party desperately needed nourishment; but the people there, at Erktrik, were hostile, and after a night in which three drivers ran off to try to get back home, the party pushed on again, reaching Owarkin, and there at last, there was plenty of food. In the nick of time, the party was saved.

Before reaching the next resting place, Areni, at Cape North, illness intensified: Harry had snow blindness and de Clinchamp had frostbite, but Areni was thankfully free of the smallpox, and some recuperation was possible. At Cape North, everything took a turn for the better, mainly because, as Harry noted, 'the natives were the friendliest we had yet seen.' Of course, the time there was not trouble-free, and this was down to drink. Harry describes a disturbing confrontation: 'A young native, having imbibed our vodka, clamoured loudly for more, and when Stepan refused, drew a knife and made a savage lunge which cut into the Cossack's furs. In an instant the aggressor was on his back in the snow.' Fortunately, the locals prevented any further trouble but Harry had his pistol drawn, ready to use.

On 19 May, they reached East Cape, two months after leaving Sredni-Kolymsk. They had covered at that point about 11,263 miles. Now, they were deeply inside Tchuktchi land. Harry took the opportunity to produce an ethnological profile, rather than dwell on past misfortune amongst these people. There is a measure of the toughness and callousness of the Tchuktchis here in Harry's profile of a man he calls 'Billy' in the narrative. Billy had joined a whaler, working out of San Francisco, and had deserted. He then lived in the area, at first prospecting for gold, which he had heard existed there. This failed, and when he met Harry's party, he was in very low spirits and physically frail. His treatment at the hands of the Tchuktchis illustrates their aggression and inability to show genuine compassion and charity. Harry and his party also had to play mind games to survive, but at least the chief of this settlement was an abstainer from alcohol, and acted in some degree as a protector, as it was when drunk that the natives of this region were murderous and violent. That chief, Teneskin, had a solid and plentiful food supply also, and agreed to supply the party with food as long as documents were signed that would entail a double repayment when the Revenue cutter came.

As with Harry's reclamation for certain death in this area in 1896, again, this cutter was what the party relied on to take them over to the shores of Alaska. In fact, a land crossing was impossible. Harry explained the problem that prevented him from actually travelling 'by land', as he had told the press, and as the title of his book promises the reader: 'The distance from shore to shore at the nearest point is about 40 miles. … Bering Straits are never completely closed, for even in midwinter, floes are on the move, which, with broad shifting "leads" of open water, render a trip on foot extremely hazardous.' Hence, the truth is that for the extent of the Bering Strait, there had been no land travel, and of course, large stretches of the expedition had been on trains. But nevertheless, the thousands of miles covered still present the reader with the reflection that taking on this journey was both brave and foolhardy – as all first attempts are.

Before the cutter, *Thetis*, finally collects the party and takes them over to Alaska, Harry gives a study of the Tchuktchis; he sees around him a breed of people who suppress their women, have no real ontology, leaving their dead out on the ice for the dogs to eat; they have no warmth towards other people and their lifestyle is one of basic, smelly humanity in dens of iniquity and (by Harry's standards) immorality. Nevertheless, he gives details of their culture and practices that would be of great interest to an anthropologist, such as their walrus hunts, their crafts, and most vividly, their lives inside their *yarats* (huts of animal skins):

At night, men, women and children stripped naked, and even then the perspiration poured off them. The nights we passed here were indescribable. Suffice it to say that in the hours of darkness in the inner chamber of that *yarat* were worthy of Dante's Inferno. And the days were almost as bad, for then the indescribable filth of the dwelling was more clearly revealed. At the daily meal we reclined on the floor … by a long platter, and lumps of walrus or seal meat were thrown at us by the hostess, whose dinner costume generally consisted of a bead necklace.

The cutter finally arrived, and the party were at last on board ship, recovering from their privations. Harry captured the mood exactly: 'And the afternoon, in that sunlit, cosy cabin, the blessed sensation of rest after toil combined with a luxurious lounge and a delicious cigar, constituted as near an approach to Nirvana as the writer is ever likely to attain on this side of the grave!'

They were now in America. He must have known that it was now a case of simply undergoing the same journey he had done a few years before, but in reverse. He would also have known that in the final part of the trip, a railway carriage awaited. Meanwhile, there was the vast land of Alaska to negotiate, and this was by steamer and skiff. Again, as with his aborted trip of 1896, Harry is much concerned to elucidate the situation in the mining camps and in the gold fields; life out there after the initial rush to find the gold by panning any area deemed to be worthwhile was the stuff of legend by this time, 1901. Harry is well aware of the media attention being paid to the rush up the Yukon. But he makes a point of bringing the myth (as in popular papers mostly) down to earth: 'There is nothing exciting or even picturesque about a modern Alaskan mining camp. Bowlers and loud checks have superseded the red flannel shirt and sombrero, and while mission libraries abound, Judge Lynch [the 'hanging judge' from Virginia] and the crack of a six-shooter are almost unknown in these townships.'

Harry himself is, naturally, a media personality also, and this affords a moment of humour; when the party reached the Fifty Mile River and a hotel in White Horse City. There, Harry read about his fame:

I took up a Seattle newspaper and carelessly glancing at the portrait of a seedy looking individual of ferocious exterior, passed it on to a neighbour – 'What a blood-thirsty ruffian.'

'Why, it is yourself!' exclaimed my friend, pointing to the heading – 'A Phenomenal Globe-Trotter', which appeared above the woodcut. I am glad to be able to add that the portrait was not from a photograph!

98

Much of the last pages of the book are concerned with railways. Harry, after all, had stated that his main reason for the trek was to ascertain the possibility of a railway from Europe to New York via Siberia and the Arctic. After experiencing the lower Yukon and the terrifying stretches of rapids, the party made it to the railhead of the White Pass Railway, and that was to take them on the last but one link in the chain of their journey. Harry makes clear the impressive nature of this engineering feat: 'As an instance of engineering skill, the White Pass is probably the most remarkable railway in existence.' When Harry and party boarded, the line was only a year old; this narrow-gauge railroad went from Whitehorse, Yukon, down to Skagway, which was a short distance north of Juneau, where Harry had stayed on his 1898 trip. The line has no connections, and was made during the first goldfield rush, completed in 1900. The Chilkoot Trail, which Harry had done before, and on which he was close to death and disaster, was now unnecessary.

This amazing construction was the work of three companies, and financed by British investment. The man responsible for the work was Michael Heney, and the work took a vast amount of explosives to make tracking possible; the narrow gauge made working with bends and crossings of deep valleys easier. This first phase of construction had not been without incident. In early 1898 the work was caught up in a confrontation involving a powerful villain known as Soapy Smith and the president of the local government, Samuel Graves. This meant that groups of vigilantes took on the criminal gang and there was eventually a gunfight at Juneau Wharf, where Soapy was killed. Work resumed, and was completed at the end of July 1900.

Once the party reached Juneau, it was then a matter of traversing the States to their destination in New York. But the railroad down to Skagway was far from comfortable, and it provided the last thrills and danger of the whole expedition, notably on one stretch:

Perhaps the worst portion of the downward journey is at a spot where solid foothold has been found impracticable, and the train passes over an artificial roadway of sleepers supported by wooden trestles and clamped to the rock by means of iron girder ... this apparently insecure structure shook so violently under the heavy weight of metal that I must own to a feeling of relief when our wheels were once more gliding over *terra firma*.

The journey was over just a small matter of 5,000 final miles by rail, first to Seattle, then to San Francisco, and finally, over to New York. Harry supplies all the data of his expedition as an addendum, and the total mileage from Paris to New York was 18,494 miles, 11,000 of which had been needed to go from Paris to the Bering Straits. The party of intrepid men reached New York on 25 August 1902. Perhaps the worst sufferer on the American part of the itinerary was the Cossack Stepan, whose wife and children were many thousands of miles back in Siberia, and of course, he faced another very long and arduous journey back home. It had taken very nearly a month to travel from Seattle to New York, given the round trip; it seems that Harry was inordinately fond of San Francisco, and had to return there before the home run.

Chapter 7

The Balkans and Russia

At odds with society, the eccentric traveller typically approached his foreign field with a more open mind than his straight-laced colleagues.

John Keay, *Eccentric Travellers*

As the new century began, Harry found himself firmly in demand for the periodicals and with a range of publishers who were keen to maximize the new opportunities for business, catering for the readers who wanted dramatic and compelling tales of derring-do. At one end of the spectrum there was Conan Doyle, who had added medieval romance and adventure to his portfolio as a writer, and in contrast, more in the realms of fact than fiction, there was Harry and writers of his ilk, who had lived to the extreme and now wrote about the experience.

In 1896, the editorship of *The Westminster Gazette* passed from its founder, E.T. Cook, to J.A. Spender. This talented and energetic journalist was to establish the journal as an organ at the very centre of the literary culture of London clubs and professional gentlemen. This happened at the very time that Harry de Windt, well-known writer, traveller and raconteur, was a regular (when not on the road) in the lounges and at the dinner tables, of a number of literary clubs. One estimate of the *Gazette*'s circulation at that time is 5,000 copies a day, and perhaps more. It certainly had power and influence amongst the liberals of Victorian Britain.

The Gazette was owned by George Newnes, the great press magnate, but Spender insisted on being left with independent control of content and authors. Stephen Koss, the historian, has summed up the journal's status: 'The stature of a journal was measured by the gratitude it received from those whom it praised, the resentment it incurred from those whom it censured, and above all – according to J.A. Spender – by the number of lesser journals that duplicated its contents.' This would be exactly the kind of outlet that Harry would have valued as he found himself, in the 1890s, as a writer in demand. After all, he had experience and expertise in several important areas of topical interest and in urgent political matters, ranging from prison reform to the radicalism in Russian society. Hence, Spender commissioned him to write a series of articles after a trip to the Balkans, which eventually became a book – *Through Savage Europe*.

Spender was just the kind of man to find Harry's writing and experience invaluable to his own enterprise. He was born in Bath in 1862, and won a classical exhibition at Balliol College, Oxford. His journalistic career began in Hull, where his uncle owned the *Eastern Morning News*; for five years in Yorkshire, John Spender learned the trade. Then the paper was sold and Spender went to London. That is where George Newnes came on the scene, as he had financed a great success with the popular paper *Tit-Bits,* and now established *The Westminster Gazette*, with Cook in charge. When Spender took over, he was keen to expand horizons and find new talent. At this time, travel was very much one of the leading genres for the better quality periodicals. It had been a feature of *The Strand*, for instance, and for *The Idler*, both doing well throughout the 1890s, and in *Harmsworth's Monthly Pictorial Magazine* and *The London Magazine* around the turn of the century, exciting and exotic locations were highly sought after by the editors for main features.

Harry also wrote for another successful journal, *The Wide World*. This was an illustrated monthly that first appeared in 1898, and was another brainchild of Newnes. The emphasis here was on *narrative*. In the 1890s that meant dangerous adventure. What took centre stage were tales of drama and risk-taking in the male world of action, enterprise and peril. In its very first edition, it puffed the feature piece as 'the most amazing story a man ever lived to tell'. This was about a man who had lived in the Australian Outback for thirty years. It was not true, but nevertheless, the spirit of the paper was absolutely right for what Harry had to offer. He knew exactly how to inject the kind of excitement and mystery into his stories that had appealed to readers of such publications as *The Boy's Own Paper* for decades, and the growing readership of young London clerks, who wanted escapist reading as they travelled to and from their desks, was only too ready to lap up Newnes's offerings.

Typical features in *The Wide World* were 'Captured by Bushmen' and 'Strange Sights in the Himalayas'. The magazine's motto was 'Truth is stranger than fiction' and the half-yearly volumes' contents were introduced by the words 'Adventure, travel, customs, sport'. Harry's Siberian journeys were serialized, and a special publication was issued in 1902, *Some Incidents of Twenty Years of Travel.* As the decade came to a close, Harry was becoming very comfortably off, and by 1910, some of his books had gone into their fifth edition.

In this context, it seemed entirely fitting that the man who had visited and seen the worst of the Russian penal system, and who had had to defend his life with a pistol in the wilds of Siberia, should be commissioned to go to a war. *Through Savage Europe* was not quite this, but still, Harry was venturing into new territory. In his preface to the second edition, he wrote with full understanding that there was an ongoing conflict and that he had a duty to report on the fundamental cultural effects of political confrontations: 'If the Balkan War has, as yet, served no other good or useful purpose, it has at any rate drawn the attention of my countrymen to easily accessible places with which, nevertheless, they were formerly as little familiar as with darkest Africa.'

By the first years of the twentieth century, after his Balkan travels, Harry had become something of an expert on Russia, and this was at a time when the Great Game had finally moved aside as bigger fish came on the scene – such as the Boer Wars and then the Balkan unrest against the Austro-Hungarian Empire, which was to lead to the Great War. It is as well to recall, at this point, before looking at Harry the traveller with a special fervour regarding the Slavic peoples, that he had played a small role in military intelligence with regard to Russia. Some background is needed here.

The backdrop to Harry's travels was the ongoing rivalry between Britain and the Russian Empire for the mastery of the great, extensive frontiers of the Far East, particularly the borderlands of India and China. Without open warfare, there had to be a so-called 'Great Game' of espionage conducted largely by junior officers. Harry, as he hints at times, was recruited to take part in some of this intelligence work. It seems clear that he did not relish the work, and he soon changed to be simply an independent traveller.

In terms of the sheer proportion of books and articles relating to military intelligence in the nineteenth century, those relating to the British Raj have always dominated. The wars in Africa attracted exceptional men, such as Baden Powell in the Matabele Wars; the Fenian activities in Canada created their charismatic figures. In the latter case, the Fenians, Irish nationalists, assembled a force in North America to plan attacks on the British land of Canada. The Indian Raj in the years c. 1840 to c. 1900 provide the military historian with almost too many narratives of discovery to cope with.

The basis of the whole business was the certainty in Whitehall that Russia had designs on extending power to India via Afghanistan. Although that meant a confrontation with a whole range of various tribal and national groups and allies, in intimidating terrain, the fears were well founded. But we have to ask why such intelligence gathering as was achieved by generations of young British officers and colonial staff was so diverse, so apparently random and lacking in a central logistical base, until 1873. In some ways, the kinds of enterprises undertaken in this context could be bizarre and eccentric, such as the brief given to the great explorer Sir Richard Burton when, as a young officer, he was sent by Sir Charles Napier to visit souks and bazaars, and one primary interest at the heart of this was a documentary interest in sexual behaviour. He discovered just to what extent British officers visited brothels and the whole affair was glossed over, with the result that Burton was sent elsewhere.

To understand exactly what the 'Game' was all about, we need to grasp the nature of the Russian ambitions towards India. The core of this expansion of their empire was gradual invasion and absorption of nations contiguous to the Russian heartland. They had thus become accustomed to coping with all kinds of ethnic diversity and were adept at taking in these new subjects of the Tsar. After all, through Britain's eyes, the Russian Empire was vast and was all in one block, unlike the British Empire, spread across the globe in clusters. Russia covered land from the border with Prussia in Europe across to Kazakhstan, and in the second half of the nineteenth century, they were to annex areas of the Uzbek territory, the city of Kokand, and the Karakum Desert, together with the Pamir Mountains.

What most irritated Britain though was the Russian desire to take the key cities of Bokhara and Khiva. These places did eventually become Russian domains. Linked to Turkestan, these two khanates were dangerously close to British India, and hence the fear of a Russian army finding its way through into the Punjab. The British Army and the army of the East India Company had coped fairly well with controlling the massive area of India and related states for over a century until the Indian Mutiny of 1857, and that was to be a notable warning to the complacency within the Raj. But Russia was going even further afield in the mid-century: Nikolai Muravev, Governor of Eastern Siberia, sent various expeditions into the far east of the continent in the 1850s and they had control of Vladivostok by 1859. Britain's sense of holding and being confident in India was severely shaken by the Mutiny, of course, and the thirty years of Great Game activities preceding that event had been largely directed by a rising paranoia about Russia 'on their patch'.

Naturally, it was also a question of the defence of British India, not merely a fear of expansion. Lieutenant Arthur Conolly (eventually murdered in 1842 by the Khan of Bokhara) had shown that it was quite possible for a Russian army to march into India by the infamous Khyber Pass, or even through Persia and Herat. Captain Abbot had explored the latter possibility also. What these journeys and their evidence of Russian potential demonstrated above all else was the absolute necessity of having in-depth knowledge of the states involved: their structures, ambitions, temperament, bellicosity and most of all perhaps, their susceptibility to bribes and blandishments.

The Russian threat had been most cogently described and argued in a publication of 1829 with the title *On the Practicability of an Invasion of British India*. This was written by Colonel George de Lacy Evans, and he estimated that it would only take the Russians three months to move from the Caspian to the Oxus, that is from Turkey to the first main river border on entry to India: the route taken by Alexander the Great in 331 BC. According to Lawrence James in his book *Raj: The Making of British India*, in 1836 there were only 17,000 British troops in India, and of these, 1,400 were invalids. Common sense dictated that a revolt would be hard to contain. The Duke of Wellington saw the heart of the problem: the nature of the native troops, the sepoys. If the British were considerate and right-thinking about the way the empire was organized in a military sense, they would ensure the support and respect for the sepoys were always there.

There were various perceptions of how the Great Game would progress at that crucially important point, c. 1840. Some considered that there would be a sudden escalation into warfare: open conflict caused by a Russian army on the move into a zone perilously close to Raj borderland. Others, largely the officers on the spot such as Abbot, Conolly and later, Sykes and Burnaby, felt sure that the Game was destined to be a relentlessly steady and uncertain series of moves, like a chess game. Whatever the course of events, one fact was certain: key buffer states would always be prime targets, notably Persia and Turkestan, and in India, the region of Sind. A typical manoeuvre in the intelligence machinations in this context was the Russian attempt to persuade the Shah in the 1830s to make a move on Heart. In the 1830s, Russia not only worked hard to influence the Shah, but also made significant advances into the possession of Kabul. The theories of de Lacy Evans must have seemed to be coming true.

Because intelligence in the mid-century, from the Crimean War to the turning point of the early 1870s, was piecemeal and *ad hoc*, it is difficult to see exactly what was going on. But there are three definite areas of interest in a general history of spies and spying in Victoria's age: the individual officers and the interplay with Russian movements; the work on the pundits and Captain Thomas Montgomerie; and the senior officers and administrators who gathered 'soldier sahibs' around them to form operational units ready to move to any part of India when an assignment occurred.

The *doyen* of Great Game studies, Peter Hopkirk, selects Lieutenant Arthur Conolly as the typical Great Game player. Conolly had been on the road for more than a year when he finally arrived in a village on the North West Frontier in 1831. He was only twenty-three years old at the time. More than this, though, is the fact that Conolly coined the phrase 'Great Game' in a letter to a friend. His main achievement was in observing the Russian army. But in order to take that enterprise to its conclusion, he had to cross the feared Karakum Desert, and that challenge exemplifies the nature of the 'Great Gamer'. The defining feature of that person is disguise. The officer going into the intelligence adventure had to become so free from his European identity that he moved, spoke and thought like a native of wherever he found himself. For those reasons, many British officers became authorities on the most obscure cultural habits and traditions of numerous tribal states and kingdoms across the continent.

If all this seems familiar, it is because Harry – and it is a topic he dodges – was one of those officers who travelled in the guise of the English gentlemen, crazy enough to slog across massive, lonely tracts of land for odd reasons. Many of such were spies, and the Russians knew it. Did Harry indulge in more espionage work for Britain than he ever lets on? It seems highly likely. He knew four languages; he could live off the land; he had a military background, since his first duties in Sarawak; and most of all, he had acquired knowledge of little-known Russia at a time when the Great Game was mounting to some kind of showdown. That it did not do so was down to a war that Russia had to stage against Japan, and that proved to be a huge diversion.

Biographers sometimes have to hazard an informed guess, and in this case, my suggestion is that Harry did his military intelligence work when he was in the Near East, as Persia and the borders of the Indian sub-continent were a 'Great Game' focus for those gentlemen and officers who were recruited for specific missions. That region entailed traversing a route that was easily utilized if a traveller wanted to make a slight digression into the war buffer zones. It was a dangerous business – one that would have suited Harry admirably. After all, just as he completed his work in Sarawak, the strategically important Russo-Turkish War took place in the late 1870s, followed by the theatre of war in Northern India. It was exactly at that period that the Russian threat from the north seemed most disturbing to Britain's military thinkers.

Whatever the truth of this, the fact is that Harry, in *Through Savage Europe* and in his writings on Russia, shows a deep interest in both the Russian army and the Tsarist regime and its opponents – and the latter extends throughout the period (roughly c. 1890 to 1917) when the radical upheavals were taking place in Russia, from assassinations to Pan-Slavic outfits, through to open revolution after the failure of a number of compromises allowed by Nicholas II.

After the debacle of the Crimean War in the 1850s, Russia had reformed and restructured its army. That new form of the military regime was crucially important to the workings of the Great Game in the East, and Harry knew that.

With this in mind, it comes as no surprise that Harry's book, *Through Savage Europe*, together with *Russia as I Know It*, which were both written about the same time, the former just before the Great War and the latter during it, present us with reflections of a man who was highly rated as an authority on matters Slavic – and with a sense of contemporary importance. In *Russia as I Know It* we have a very odd publication: reaching its fifth edition in 1917, it presents remarkable assessments of the Russian army as well as strong opinions of what were known then as 'Nihilists' – a term used in Europe for any kind of Russian radical. The fifth edition was written with the publishers clearly seeing the opportunity of explaining Britain's allies in the Great War, particularly as there had been the decisive defeat of the Russian army by the Germans at the opening of the war, from 20 to 31 August 1914. Two great Russian armies had moved into East Prussia, the second into an area south of the Masurian Lakes. Incompetence in the leadership had led to a defeat that entailed the loss of 125,000 men and 500 guns.

Harry's work provided an assessment of the reforms that the Russian army had experienced, first after their success in the Russo-Turkish War of the 1870s, and then after the defeat of the Russians in the war against Japan in the last years of the nineteenth century. Harry is very adept at explaining the workings and nature of the Russian army during a thirty-year period, and built into this is an element that reads like sheer, open propaganda for an ally in need of a boost:

> But anyway, Russia has now become our staunch friend and ally, wherefore it is satisfactory to reflect that, except on two occasions, she has never met with what can be called a really decisive defeat. On the other hand, she successfully resisted Napoleon for years, and eventually drove him out of the country with heavy loss; while in 1878 she completely routed the Turks, and would, if not restrained by the Powers, have annexed Constantinople.

The assessment of the 'nihilist' is an odd read, when we bear in mind that, as the account was first written in 1910, Russia was going through the major crisis of the Dumas, following the failed revolution of 1905. There were four Dumas (parliaments) from 1906 to 1914, which had emerged from the Tsar's realization of the depth of the opposition to his rule, and in this sequence of short assemblies, the Tsar's henchman, Stolypin, had applied a repressive regime in which the Okhrana (secret police) and the imperial army had murdered large numbers of radicals. Harry had met many of the intelligentsia who had been exiled to Siberia, so he knew their attitudes and the reasons for their punishment, but oddly, he skips of that political subject and keeps to what he knows, perpetuating a rather mythical, media-created image of the Socialist thinkers who desperately wanted a new way of ruling Russia, without the Romanov tsars. He wrote, for instance, with facile generalizations, and with the attitudes of a reactionary: 'But a fairly long and varied experience has shown me that Socialism, in Russia, is in many cases taken up by young and impulsive people as a fad.' He also adds the usual Victorian condemnation of radicalism that links uncleanliness with amorality: 'The revolutionary youth of both sexes in Russia are easily recognized, for the men affect an eccentric style of dress, wear their hair very long, and are rather chary of soap and water; while even young and attractive women cut off their luxuriant tresses and display an utter indifference as to their personal appearance.'

Russia as I Knew It has the hallmark of a publication eagerly put before the public at a time when a boost was required in the mindset of the Allies against the Central Powers; reading it, we see a writer who should have kept to the domain of documentary and reportage rather than offering something that would give readers a topical interpretation of the world-shaking events happening in Russia as the book went to press. The saving grace of the book, however, is the assessment of the Russian army reforms, which, bearing in mind what has been said about the winding down of the Great Game, does give a reason why that ongoing war of plans and counter-plans thinned out by the 1890s. For instance, his words on the earlier reforms after the defeats in the Crimea (in the 1850s) do point to important changes such as better educated officers and more attainable promotion for men of the lower *moujik* class (roughly, equivalent to lower middle class in English terms). But again, propaganda and half-truths step in when he allots great praise to Tsar Nicholas II for army reforms. These did happen, but for the security of the Romanov rule rather than for any altruistic or even concessional reasons that might have reduced the ranks of the opposition that was eventually to lead to his ruin and death in 1917.

Harry returned to safer ground in his next work *Through Savage Europe*, and this time, he was fully aware of the civil and military strike that was shaking that region as he went there, once more attracted to a certain degree of risk and peril. He went there just a few years before the dissent against the dominance of the Austro-Hungarian Empire ceased to be simply a festering resentment and exploded, of course, with the assassination of the Archduke Franz Ferdinand. The book is still very much a mix of a gentleman's travel guide and a piecemeal assessment of the politics and the military powers found in that area. Yet there is a new dimension too – he was, in part, a war correspondent.

There were several war correspondents at work in the time of Harry's early life and writing career: Archibald Forbes, Charles Norris-Newman and Melton Prior. But there were also many writers from the local papers in war zones. Few wars have been so thoroughly reported – in this case, very much by locals in the Natal newspapers as well as by Forbes and Norris-Newman – as the Zulu War of 1879 and the earlier Crimean War, written up by Russell of *The Times*. Harry would be well aware of this profession, and he knew some of these men. In terms of how they related to the fluid intelligence of imperial wars, the central point is that they were supportive of the British officer and they tried to understand his viewpoint on things. In the end, their purpose was to produce copy that would be exciting and dramatic to read – narratives that would form part of the ongoing story of how the empire was being won and retained. But in Harry's case, he wasn't even among British officers.

Along with the writers came the special artists: notably, Melton Prior of *The Illustrated London News* and Charles Fripp of *The Graphic*. Visual records are especially important in the history of military intelligence, in the localized area of work, because they had a documentary aspect in the Victorian age. They were particularly open to being accused of espionage, as in the case of war artist William Simpson, famous for his work in Crimea, who was arrested in Germany at Metz in 1870 on suspicion of being a spy. Most drawings give detailed and accurate images of warriors and battle scenes, terrain and resources. They were the kinds of notations that had been done for decades by the writer-travellers into Asia. Charles Norris-Newman's work also has a significance in this documentary aspect: he was there from the start of Chelmsford's advance against the Zulu, being attached to the 3rd Natal Native Contingent in the Third Column. His writing and the illustrations in his book *In Zululand with the British Throughout the War of 1879* exemplify the best elements of the documentary method in that age of fact gathering. He wastes no time in that work in offering a concise explanation of the weakness in the campaign: 'They, however, greatly miscalculated the power of their new foe.'

Then, in the European wars, since the 1870 Franco-Prussian War in particular, literary men had increasingly been given briefs to enter and write about all kinds of war zones. Spenser Wilkinson had shown the way, not long before Harry's trip to Russia and the Balkans; he had actually been suspected of being a spy and was arrested. Clearly, Harry was aware of these risks, as he comments on the camera, being publicly used by Mackenzie, and he makes a point of assessing military capabilities in every state that he visits.

Now there he was – the well-known traveller and one-time spy – trekking across the unstable, risky Balkan landscape at a time when insurrection was in the air. Another journalist of some fame at the time, Max Pemberton, who also went to the Balkans about the same time as Harry, describes what Harry was to see:

> The wild Balkans are not wild today as they were in 1900. Many of the great forests are virgin forests no longer. You do not see, as I saw, bears playing on the hillside. Murderers are not let out of prison for the day so that they may make music for you – as they were for us at Jezero. You do not enter mountain towns through gates that have known Mohammed. Regiments of cavalry are not marched through hills that your journey may be safe. All these things happened to our little party and left us grateful.

This could almost be a summary of what Harry was about to experience. But often he was on his own, and that makes a difference. Pemberton's memory is of a guided tour: Harry went with his hand always not far from his pistol.

The subject of maps now needs some consideration. Previous to this expedition, Harry, having been a member of the Royal Geographical Society since 1890, had had access to the resources of that society. Harry was proposed by Thomas Fuller, a member, who recommended him from personal knowledge, and this was backed by George H. Richards and James Andrews. He was proposed on 10 February and elected on 28 April that year. His name was removed from the RGS lists in 1925, which almost certainly meant that he was not keeping up his subscription payments.

At this time, Harry was living at 58 Jermyn Street, which had been rebuilt quite recently, in 1880. It was a single block, with a tailor's shop in the basement and on the first floor, and flats on the other floors. One description notes that there were 'three widely spaced windows to each story' and that there were balconies with wrought iron railings; the doors had a large cornice hood. A publication of 1932 describes the area: 'To a large extent Jermyn Street is a backwater of Piccadilly, inasmuch as several large buildings have frontages to this street and various shabby houses at the corner of Wells Street have recently given way to modern buildings.' The street is placed between Piccadilly and Pall Mall, and in Harry's time he would have been close to the theatres and the best restaurants. It was an area full of tailors and gents' outfitters; the tailor to the Rothschilds, Cesare Salvucci, lived there, and in 1907, Alfred Dunhill opened his tailoring business there. It seems entirely fitting, given that Harry was described as a 'gentleman' when he joined the RGS, that today a statue of Beau Brummell stands in Jermyn Street. It was, in short, the residence of a wealthy gentleman who loved to be near the pleasures and conveniences of his ways of life, from the clubs to the outfitters and theatres.

Since the escalation of foreign travel for scholarly as well as for recreational reasons, the RGS had expanded its facilities and support networks. In 1883 it formed an Instruments Committee, and throughout the period 1877 to 1900, it has been calculated that they loaned equipment to 186 expeditions. Maps were also being produced, and this had always been one of the first initiatives of the Society. In 1878, the administrators decided that relevant maps would be given out to members at evening meetings. By 1903, the Society published its own general guide, *Hints to Travellers*. The guiding light in this period was Sir Clements Markham, who was RGS Secretary from 1863 to 1888, and then was President at the time of Harry's main journeys. His most characteristic statement was, 'The first work of geographers is to answer the question, *where is it*?' Markham had a special interest in Antarctic exploration, and he wanted this to be undertaken by the navy. But this is not to say that he did not encourage travel by amateurs and gentlemen. Like Harry, he was always busy either travelling or writing about his journeys.

The *Hints to Travellers*, as Nicholas Murray notes in his anthology of Victorian travellers, *A Corkscrew is Most Useful*, contained the products of experience, and he quotes the words of John Kirk, who went with Livingstone: 'When Dr Livingstone and I crossed the mountains and reached Lake Shirwa, our outfit was as follows: one pocket chronometer, two prismatic compasses, one pocket compass, one field-glass, one aneroid barometer, two common thermometers,' along with 'arsenical soap' and 'botanical paper'. This was a tradition in guidebooks and travel books that Harry was to learn from: he made a habit of stressing the need to travel light, and he also provided lists of absolutely essential luggage. There is no doubt that Harry wanted to succeed by dumping most of the trappings of 'tourist' travel.

By 1905, when preparing for the Balkans, Harry now had the firm of Collins Bartholomew behind him. This company was at first based in Edinburgh, founded about 1826 by John Bartholomew. His son, John Ian Bartholomew, was running the company when Harry went to the Balkans, and it has been claimed that the firm prepared no less than 2,000 sheets of maps for Harry in October 1903. This is hard to believe, as so few maps are actually used in his works, but it seems more likely that the company, along with the RGS, provided maps for use on the expeditions rather than for printing.

In the last decade of the nineteenth century and into the Edwardian years, map-making became more sophisticated and approachable; even school textbooks show a very high standard. Both Philips and Bartholomew produced exceptionally clear and detailed maps, and the handbooks on geography show an impressive summation of the knowledge acquired by travellers such as Harry. A school book of 1908, for instance, published by Philips, has a concise, factual account of Siberia, produced just a few years after the opening of the Trans–Siberian Railway.

The 1905 Balkan journey was very current too. The little-known regions in that area – such as Herzegovina or Bosnia – were very little understood, and their identity was rather closer to the fictional Ruritania and the world of Anthony Hope's novels than to any semblance of reality. Franz Lehar's operetta, *The Merry Widow*, set in the imaginary state of Pontevedro, was first performed in Vienna at the end of 1905, and was on tour across Austria in 1906 as Harry was travelling. The image of Pontevedro there is one of soldiers elaborately dressed, after the fashion of Austrian military costume, but in the operetta, the entire context is of 'chocolate box soldiers' and of aristocrats full of their own importance.

The RGS had a particular interest in exploration to the Near and Far East at this time. A survey of some of their meetings indicates this, as can be seen for instance in a meeting of 1891, when member Sir M.E. Grant-Duff spoke on 'Travel and ascents to the Basarjuri District, Daghestan', and Mr Douglas Freshfield spoke on exploration and photography in a trip to the Caucasus. In that he was a precursor to Harry, who had Mackenzie and his biography for exactly the same reason. Baker also stressed what Harry was to stress, that the area 'had long been a field for romance and robbery.' At the RGS anniversary meeting in June that same year, it was announced that there were 3,579 Fellows of the Society and that although, in the words of the Secretary, the year 'had not been a successful or brilliant one' the net income for the previous year had been over £9,000. The Society was thriving. Their publication, *The Geographical Magazine*, had a circulation of 1,500 at the time. Harry had immense resources at the turn of the century, from the RGS and from Bartholomew's.

Interest in the Balkans went along concurrently, and in spite of the frequent political upheavals there, Baedeker produced his guide to Austria-Hungary in 1906, although Thomas Cook had not ventured there yet.

Harry's book includes a 'Balkan War Map', and this shows his itinerary: he started on the Adriatic coast at Montenegro and crossed steadily to the Black Sea and to his favourite subject for writing – Russia. His interest is, as usual, often in hotels, meals and good company, but he shows his special skill in this work in describing local habits and culture. But even in his first impressions he shows an awareness of some of the urgent contemporary issues in Balkan societies, such as emigration and brigandage. Regarding the latter, it needs to be stressed that the general reputation the Balkans at that time had for piracy and robbery may have been exaggerated in popular cultural narratives, but it had a basis in fact. The Balkan states had been under the control of Turkey's vast Ottoman Empire for centuries, and as one specialist historian on the area explained, under the Ottomans, 'revived the extended family and the importance of kinship and clan associations such as the South Slav "zadruga", especially in remote, rugged, highland and frontier areas.'

There may not have been the pirates in 1905, but Harry witnessed a casualty of a vendetta. As he was watching a street scene in Cettigne, Montenegro, 'Suddenly ... a shot rang out, fired from a horse pistol, to judge by the deafening sound of the report. ... I joined in a stampede to an even more densely crowded portion. ... It was impossible to approach the spot or ascertain the cause of the disturbance until a lane was cleared ... through it appeared a limp, lifeless form, carried on a wooden shutter. ... I could only catch a glimpse of a white, blood-stained face'.

In the background history, the question of emigration was a massive influence. There had been a population explosion throughout the mid-century, and emigration soared. One history of the area gives some figures: 'Between 1876 and 1915, more than 319,000 Greeks, 92,000 Romanians, 80,000 Bulgarians and 1,380 Serbs emigrated to other continents.' Harry, as he always does, expands on this trend by noting a remarkable example:

Dalmatia is a productive country, but its resources are being less developed year by year on account of the increasing emigration of the natives to the United States, to which Great British and German liners from Trieste convey them at

> absurdly low rates. … A strong incentive to emigration is the
> beautiful palace built here by a Dalmatian peasant who went
> to America twenty years ago, struck oil, and returned three
> years ago to his native country a millionaire!

Harry was writing in the context of a dark new world of international
terrorism where assassination was reported almost every week in the
popular papers. He would have been well aware that even in politically
stable Britain, there had been numerous attempts on the life of Queen
Victoria throughout her long reign. Drawings and postcards show the
British Royal Family attending functions and travelling through
London streets in open-backed carriages, open to any crackpot with a
revolver. There had been Fenian activity too, notably in the bombing
of Clerkenwell House of Correction in 1867. When he travelled to the
Balkans, he knew that the little states, mostly under the control of the
Austro-Hungarian Empire, were riddled with activists, and he knew
that there was a gun culture in these places, along with a high level of
violent crime. If he wanted danger, he was not disappointed.

Around the time he was in the Balkans, 1905–06, Harry would
have read in the news that in Russia there were murders of politicians
and officials; a bomb had exploded in the Bois de Vincennes, Paris,
and in Holland there was an Anarchist Congress, where members
argued over the differing agendas of anarchists and syndicalists. On 1
August 1905, the Aliens Act was passed in Britain, and 9 January was
'Bloody Sunday' in St Petersburg, when a petition signed by 135,000
people was to be presented to the Tsar, asking for reform. Troops fired
into the crowd and 150 people were killed. In this atmosphere, Harry
went into the interior of that bundle of small states from which the
Great War would begin – the outcome of yet another political
assassination, when Gavrilo Princip, a Bosnian student, shot the
Archduke Franz Ferdinand in Sarajevo, where Harry had been
drinking and chatting a few years before.

Harry's journey through 'savage Europe' does indeed recount
savagery. Aware of the current upheavals caused by political
radicalism, he makes dramatic use of assassination stories from Serbia

(then known as 'Servia') and in his chapter on 'murderers in uniform' he wrote as powerful an account of a horrendous slaughter as will be found in any popular history. This was the killing of King Alexander and Queen Draga of Serbia in June 1903. Other officials died with them, and the actual murder, after the gang of drunken officers sprayed gunfire around at random, was a merciless shooting and mutilation of the royals after they were found hiding in a clothes closet. Harry makes this a prolonged and exciting narrative.

Woven into the story is Harry's interest in divination, and he cannot resist this: 'At the Queen's request, Draga's hand by a cheiromant (palm reader) who predicted that its owner would one day attain an illustrious position but that then her life would be in the direst peril.' We may believe this or not, but it led to the dreadful tale that Harry tells at great length, never letting the intensity and the sense of fear slacken until the horrible climax in the private royal rooms:

> Draga was cowering in the corner shaking with terror, while the King, revolver in hand, tried to shield her person from the gaze of the brutal intruders. Colonel Maschin [leader of the killers] was the first to stride up to the King with a document for his signature – a promise to banish Draga for ever or to abdicate. Alexander made no reply, but fired point-blank at the speaker – missing him – upon which a volley fired by his companions laid the King low. … It was now Draga's turn and the wretched woman begged so piteously for mercy that her screams were heard in the main street.

In this narrative voice we may detect the writer for the new adventure periodicals, but this was hard, contemporary fact, and it reached out emotionally to the greater story – now international – of the fear of anarchy and the decline of monarchies.

Harry and his party were not immune from attack either while in Serbia, and they had an experience that was the stuff of nightmares. They had stopped at Nisch, where the Orient Express stopped, and where the hotels were decent and comfortable, and had then pressed on, travelling on a country cart, and one of their stops was at a place called Ropitza. Harry commented that this village 'contained as tough a crowd of ruffians as it has ever been my lot to encounter … Ropitza has an evil reputation, for it is the favourite meeting place of thieves, smugglers and shady characters from all parts of the Balkans.' He was in deep water, but didn't realize it until after they had gone on to the road again, their driver being tipsy with slivovitch (damson spirit). There was a 'violent lurch' and the driver was thrown on to the road. In front was a pine tree, blocking their path, and then came what must have been one of Harry's most fearful experiences:

> I turned hastily to discover perhaps twenty silent, shadowy forms, which had apparently sprung out of the earth around us. There was no 'Your money or your life' business about this strange band but its methods were quite as effectual. 'You will give us 200 dinaras and we will help you shift that tree. … Resistance was, of course, useless, for a match was kindled by the speaker ostensibly to light a cigarette, but probably to reveal the gleam of firearms in every man's belt.

The sum demanded was only, in sterling, eight pounds. But Harry and friends were lucky that the robbers did what they said they would do. Harry adds, with characteristic relish for astounding facts, 'For we afterwards ascertained that a dozen persons had been waylaid and robbed (one of them being murdered) on this road within the past year.'

When Harry and party moved on to Bulgaria, there was another puzzling piece of political power that needed to be assessed. Again, Harry provided an account of this, centring on the ruler, Prince Ferdinand I, at a momentous time for the nation, as on 5 October 1908 (when Harry was back home) he proclaimed Bulgaria's independence from the Ottoman Empire, stating that Bulgaria was then a kingdom, rather than a constituent state, with himself as Tsar.

The Ottoman Empire, controlled by the Porte in Turkey (the government body) had been in existence since the thirteenth century, when Osman became the first empire builder. Over time, it expanded, so that it controlled land from the Crimean Sea to Algiers, and most of the Balkan nations, right up to the fringes of Austrian land. At the Berlin Congress of 1878, Serbia, Montenegro and Romania had been made independent, while Bosnia and Herzegovina were absorbed into the Austro-Hungarian Empire. The Balkan Wars of 1912–13, just after Harry's trip, were a joint attempt by the remaining states, including Bulgaria, to throw off the Ottoman yoke. After the Great War, the Ottoman lands were finally fragmented and new nations emerged as the Near East reshuffled and fresh geographical boundaries were established.

Harry was there, to assess Ferdinand, on the very edge of the Revolution. Ferdinand was born in Vienna in 1861, and was in the Saxe-Coburg-Gotha dynasty (the same as the monarchs of Britain). He grew up in Slovakia, acquiring the culture and mindset of the Austro-Hungarian rulers. His father, Augustus, was a first cousin of Queen Victoria. In 1887, Ferdinand took his place in Bulgaria, and one comment about him was that he was totally unfit for the role. In the 1890s, there had been a crisis in Bulgaria's relations with Russia, which was always important to those in Russia who wanted a pan-Slavonic unity of states, largely because of a politician called Stefan Stambolov, and when he was assassinated in 1894, Ferdinand was at the reins of power.

Harry's assessment of Ferdinand is in line with British thinking at the time: 'Prince Ferdinand is certainly not popular, which is partly owing to the fact that he is away for more than two-thirds of the year, and that even when in Bulgaria he chiefly resides in one of his country palaces.' Harry saw that Stambolov had exerted a degree of restraint, but that since his death, Ferdinand had become an over-indulged potentate. Harry summed up the situation neatly: 'There is no doubt that Prince Ferdinand's rule in Bulgaria hangs by a thread. ... The reigning Prince is not a clever man ... Stambolov, one of the greatest men Bulgaria has ever produced, almost despised him.'

Harry characterizes Bulgaria as 'the land of unrest' and as usual, he set great store by the evidence of military strength. On looking at an army review, he was impressed, and he opined that the Bulgarian fighters were notably fierce. He summed up:

On my return home I was asked by an English general if Prince Ferdinand could put 100,000 men into the field at a month's notice, and he seemed incredulous when I told him that in that space of time Bulgaria could mobilize a well-equipped and efficient force of half a million men.

In the capital, Sofia, Harry met a newspaper editor whom he trusted as a reliable source of up-to-date information on the place; one outstanding aspect of life he found there was the nature of the intelligentsia. He saw that a university was being built, but that Bulgarians of any wealth and status sent their children to Europe for their education. Still, he found there a reading culture, commenting, 'Sofia alone has nearly a score of daily and weekly publications – one or two of them illustrated – and the latter, though poor productions, are creditable enough when we consider the age (or rather youth) of this go-ahead little country.'

That patronizing tone is a feature of Harry's tendency when summing up a place or a particular culture, and it has to be said that he was typical of his age and class in that habit. Also, as Harry always had a penchant for detecting the underbelly of any location with a facile appearance of style and modernity, he leaves Bulgaria with a comment on the sewage: 'I should mention one drawback connected with this city, and that is its deplorable drainage, which often causes serious epidemics.'

Harry and party then moved on to a place that resonates through European history – Plevna. This was the site of a great siege during the Russo-Turkish War 0f 1877–78. The Ottoman (Turkish) forces held their ground against the might of Russia for five months, and that allowed time for other small states to join the Turks. The casualties were high: 40,000 killed or wounded. It had happened largely because the Russian commander, Grand Duke Nicholas, had advanced without resistance to this strategically important spot before the Turkish leader, Osman, could act. But just in time, the Turks made a strongly defensible position and a sequence of four battles followed. At the final battle, in the Shipka Pass, the Russian leader, General Gourko, finally won the day for the Russians, but the Turks' resistance had won them a high reputation across Europe.

Harry and party travelled by train, and it was not a comfortable journey to Plevna, which he found to be 'a sleepy little town' where he wasted no time in finding a veteran of the battle to ask about the famous confrontation. Harry found an old Chevalier Garde, who furnished him with this account about Osman Pasha:

'I can see him now … that marvellous man, refusing to yield up his sword to the Prince of Rumania (whom he regarded as a rebel) and handing it to our General as though he were granting a favour! … We found Osman in a squalid hovel with a mud floor, lit by a broken window stuffed up with bits of rag. … Everyone was shivering except the hero of Plevna, who, however, was deadly pale from exhaustion and from physical pain for his leg was being bandaged.'

Then the rain fell, and Harry had to endure a torrent. But he was still impressed by the Bulgarian people, and the weather gave him time to stop and study them. He noted: 'It is a paradise of greenery and vegetation … the peasantry looked prosperous and well-to-do.' The party moved on to Gabrova, and then to the Shipka Pass, where the nature of the great battle really hit home. By the time they planned the trip to Gabrova, it was no longer a train journey, but a *troika* trip (a Russian vehicle pulled by a team of three horses).

The Balkans Harry travelled through was undoubtedly an imminent fissure waiting to split in the great structure of Europe. Only a few years after Harry returned, the situation was transmuted from rumbling discontent to open war. The historian J.A.S. Grenville sums up this cataclysm:

Other European nations with their own ambitions added to the breakdown of stability in the Balkans. The Ottoman Empire was attempting to reform itself after the Young Turk revolution of 1908. But Turkey was weak. Italy attacked Turkey in 1911 and annexed Tripoli. The small Balkan states, equally greedy, wanted Turkish territory in Europe and were ready to fight each other over the spoils. Turkish weakness, Balkan nationalism, and the rivalry of Austria and Russia destabilized south-east Europe.

Harry and friends had crossed these lands just a few years before, and he had sensed the discontent and, at times, actually encountered the 'savagery' he expected to find there.

The journey progressed into Romania, and the book became a mix of a 'travelogue' style at times, along with something far more interesting – a battlefield experience. The reader will recall, in the chapter on Bucharest, that Harry wrote about a 'city of pleasure' and he highlights those aspects. But in the journey through the Shipka Pass, we have a very vivid and insightful narrative of what the struggle in that high pass must have been like in 1877:

The Shipka Pass is nearly 5,000 feet above sea level, and it took us several hours to reach the summit, for the road was very rough and in places partly broken away. From here there is a magnificent view, and this is perhaps the only object in ascending the fatal pass where, in 1877, almost as many perished from blinding blizzards and the ferocious cold as from shot and shell. We visited the granite obelisk and little burial ground which mark the last resting place of many a brave Russian and Bulgarian, and faintly realized as we toiled wearily up to the rocky peak what a similar ascent must have meant under a hail of shell and shrapnel.

In Bucharest, Harry is at home. The place was known as the Paris of the Balkans, and he tended to agree. He reports that the land is a 'new and progressive kingdom', and he is once more impressed by the military capabilities of King Carol I's forces. But what is obvious through the whole experience of Romania is Harry's tribute to the luxury around him in the hotels and in the cafés and restaurants. He noted that the Hotel Splendide, 'in this city of 300,000 souls, is considered the best' but that 'a prolonged residence would tax a millionaire's resources.' He always did relish the life of the boulevards and taking tea in places where civilized conversation was valued, and he found these in Bucharest.

In that city, his trip for *The Westminster Gazette* was almost over. Just before the Russian border, his companion Mackenzie left him, the reason being that 'the presence of a bioscope artist in a disturbed city might produce unpleasant results.' Harry was on familiar ground now, moving on to Odessa and Rostov.

Once more alone, Harry, in the last stretch of Romania before entering Russia, was in for some trials of endurance. He reported that the trouble began at a place called Ungheni, where all travellers were subjected to a thorough search. The security was intense: 'A passport was not sufficient, for every traveller was rigidly cross-examined as to his antecedents and business in the country.' At last he boarded a train and was bound for Odessa, but still the disturbances and inconveniences continued, as there had been a riot nearby, and when the train arrived in Odessa, there was a regiment of troops standing to. The pressures continued when he went into town: 'While in Odessa I was subjected to an incessant police espionage.' But, as we learn, Harry actually had a mission. Although he was on his commission from the journal back in London, he had not forgotten his Russian connections made in Siberia some years before.

This was, in truth, a foolhardy objective, and he was risking being arrested. He was aiming to contact the brother of a political exile he knew in Siberia; that would have made him a suspicious character in the eyes of the Russian Okhrana. He was justifiably nervous: 'I need not describe the ruses and risks which had been resorted to and run in order to accomplish my mission,' he wrote. Even in his hotel, he was warned not to go anywhere near public buildings or government offices. He soon discovered that the official precautions were wise: he witnessed an attempted assassination. Harry described the event:

The afternoon was bright and sunny, and the Deribasovka [Deribasovskaya], a fashionable thoroughfare, crowded with people. Suddenly the report of a pistol, closely followed by another, caused a number of people to rush to the spot where an elderly man in the official uniform of grey and scarlet had fallen to the ground. My policeman [who had stopped him earlier] now heedless of cameras, made also off like a flash of lightning to render assistance, and I discreetly and rapidly followed his example – in the opposite direction.

Harry's final task for his editor back home was to create a profile of that crucially important Russian city; he made sure that his readers were told about the Black Sea and about the impressive Nikolaevsky Boulevard, which Harry saw as 'one of the finest in Europe'.

He was soon on board a train again, travelling to Rostov. The Harry depicted here is a far cry from the man slogging through Siberia; he reported that he enjoyed 'fresh caviar, soup, starlet, a partridge, beautifully cooked and served, and at a cost of only two roubles, or four shillings, including coffee and a bottle of Crimean claret'. On arrival he noted that everyone was eating sunflower seeds, and he fancifully put the feeling of cheerfulness he sensed down to the food.

The journey ended after a brief stop at Ekaterinoslav, 'the Birmingham of Southern Russia', as he called it, and a final trip into the Caucasus on the way to Warsaw, where he would take a train homewards. His last report is from Vladikavkaz, and as an extra excursion was made impossible by the lack of post horses, he lingered in Vladikavkaz, and as things turned out, he did well to enjoy its relaxing charms because, after a smooth journey to Warsaw, once again Harry de Windt seemed to attract danger. There was a riot, and the noise woke him up in his hotel bed.

Warsaw was at the time one of the main cities of the Russian Empire, with well over half a million inhabitants; the Tsar and his government were then pressing forward the 'Russification' of the empire, and Polish nationalism was in a struggle for existence against the authorities. When trouble stirred, in came the regiments of Don

Cossacks, to apply tough suppression of dissent. The main Polish focus of aggressive opposition to the Russian Empire was led by Józef Piłsudski, who had gathered a strong fighting force. In 1906 they undertook small but effective acts of resistance and defiance, such as in 1908, when they held up a Russian mail train. In 1908, Pilsudski formed the Association for Armed Struggle, and in 1912, he led the Rifleman's Association, who were to be 12,000 strong by 1914. In 1905, just as Harry arrived to begin his Balkan journey, Piłsudski's nationalist party was the largest in the whole of the Russian Empire. Harry must have known that when his train pulled into Warsaw, he was deeply enmeshed in the street war that grew from this ongoing struggle.

There is nothing quite like the description we have in this work, which compares with any of his writing elsewhere, when he deals with responses to horror or extreme suffering. After a full day of intermittent rioting, exploding bombs and police repression, Harry takes a stroll outside his Warsaw hotel and he sees a wagon arrive, with something under cover. He walks to the building, then offers some money to persuade an officer to let him go inside, and witnesses something that will give him immoveable traumatic images for the rest of his life. This was the scene:

> Men and women lay almost over one another in the confined space, dressed in the clothes in which they had met their end a few hours before, but both sexes were stripped to the waist. … Some were shockingly disfigured, having been clubbed to death with the butt ends of rifles, but many of the women had been shot in the back while trying to reach a place of safety. … The victims appeared to be chiefly poor people. … The work of identification was to take place early the next morning.

Harry ends his book with this scene, and concludes, 'I have had to witness other ghastly scenes in the darkest recesses of the Tsar's great Empire, but the recollection of that dark cellar, with its rows of upturned staring faces, will haunt me to my dying day.' This is an amazingly candid and heartfelt passage, and it comes at the closure of a strange book, one that sits uneasily between genres. But there is no denying that in the last three chapters of *Through Savage Europe*, Harry de Windt takes on the role of war correspondent. He was there to write features, and the result was that, but also something more: he was writing reportage, and from the thick of the trouble. Even as his train pulled away from Warsaw, a bullet slammed into the window of the next carriage.

It had been a typical example of a war correspondent's experience. The 'travelogue' feel of the opening had very little to do with the mood at the end of his journey.

Chapter 8

The Clubman: Literary Friendships

From before the time of my marriage, in 1879 ... I was, I
am afraid, more given to club life than was justifiable in
a man of domestic habits and tastes.

Frank Archer, *An Actor's Notebooks*

Harry de Windt, seen throughout London and the literary world as the
man you wanted for a talk, a lecture or simply a solidly entertaining
dinner table raconteur, was the ideal clubman. That type may be hard
to define. In 1950, a publication produced by the Whitbread group,
which had a vested interest in the survival of gentlemen's clubs, tried
to define the anonymous writer called 'the clubbish animal' and part
of that definition is the man who 'attempts at getting away for a while,
from his relatives.' In Harry's case, there is some truth in that. He was
hardly the typical family man of his time, and in spite of his three
marriages, he was a man's man, who longed for the talk and the
comradeship of other men; hence his membership of several London
clubs.

The London club in about 1880: the very words bring to mind
leather armchairs, servants with silver trays and brandy; roaring coal
fires; games of cards and talk of the likely Derby winner or the batting
form of the opener for Surrey. This was a little world of men,
somewhere between a cosy home and a business forum, but even those
two notions fail to capture the essence of the literary club at the time.
This is because it was not merely a place: it was an *idea*.

The club itself was a place where a man of the arts or of the pen
could answer correspondence, broker a deal for a provincial tour, or sell
a new novel to a rising publisher eager for kudos and status among the
empires of Smith and Mudie, with their railway station bookstalls, and

publishing magnates such as Chapman and Hall or the grand, enviable John Murray and Constable, who had seen the greats into print.

If we want to understand the club as it would have been when motor cars were just about to be imagined and flying machines still on the drawing boards, we have to imagine a day in the life of Mr Corney Grain, lawyer and piano entertainer, and close friend of Harry. Corney was large, rotund: very much in the girth and character of G.K. Chesterton. He was a reliable defence lawyer to call upon, and his name is scattered through the sessions paper records of the Old Bailey. But he was also an immensely popular piano entertainer, and just after Christmas in 1889 he wrote a hasty note to a Mrs Robertson:

BEEFSTEAK CLUB

I could come February 15th (Saturday) 1890. Would the trains arrive at Broxbourne at 7.36 pm it would give me time to get something to eat after my work.
Most kind regards
R. Corney Grain

How he would have loved a mobile phone, but the best he could do was call a servant at the Beefsteak, where all the best theatre people gathered, and scribble the essential information to his client. He was wanted at a house party, and his first thought was for his stomach, and how to please it in between the duties of attending to legal cases and playing the ivories.

At the very heart of his life was the Beefsteak. There he could relax amongst bachelors such as himself, or among married men who were playing at being bachelors while in refuge from their wives. Corney's club was an address, of course: he could be *found* there. But often, gentlemen did not wish to be found, but rather forgotten in their time in that replacement for the alma mater of college or from a place of business, which would have been decidedly a male province.

The ladies were to follow, though, after the Great War, as evidenced by reading the literary memoirs and gossip of the years between the eighties and the suffragette activism of Edwardian times.

Marie Belloc Lowndes, sister of Hilaire Belloc, moved in the literary circles of that time, rubbing pens with most of the celebrities of her day. After 1918, she was a member of the Thirty Club, which met around the corner from Selfridges in Audley Street. They were originally women working in the new advertising industry, but literary and artistic women joined in. Incidentally, Harry's sister, the Ranee, was known to visit the clubs, and dined with Marie Belloc Lowndes when she was in London. Such was the small world of London's glitterati.

These institutions figure prominently in the history of writing and publishing, and had done so long before 1880, but the added interest of the arrival of the *nouveaux riche* in the last decades of Victoria's time deepens the interest somewhat. The new men were building their city mansions and country seats and their wealth had given them *entrée* to the exclusive locations of the men who ran the empire and the rich men's playgrounds of the age.

Clubs existed for particular professions, or for common hobbies and enthusiasms; they often existed to extend the leisure activities of sporting types or academics. Whatever their bias or preference, guests were welcome, and dinners were at the heart of the experience. A dinner around the end of the century might have more courses than the number of rooms in the building; simply sitting down to eat was a tacit agreement that a massive quantity of entertaining talk or attentive listening could be guaranteed. If there was a speaker (which there often was) then the ritual, with all its fun, could be further intensified. Toasts and hearty vows of a political or scurrilous nature could spice the occasion too.

Harry was typical of his time in being a member of several clubs. Writers and artists in Victoria's reign mixed in a number of clubs; it was essential to be seen and known, and London never slept. George Augustus Sala, a journalist writing in 1858, described London 'twice round the clock' – explaining he hungered for socializing and entertainment at all hours of the day and night. Sala explained the vast spectrum of clubs available, listing eighteen of them, adding that 'Clubbism is a great mystery, and its adepts must be cautious how they explain its shibboleth to the outer barbarians. Men have been expelled from clubs ere now for talking or writing about another member's whiskers.'

Yet some men gravitated to a club and never shifted allegiance. George Grossmith, the first great star of the Savoy Operas and author with his brother of *The Diary of a Nobody*, was introduced to club life by his father, also George Grossmith. George Senior was a dedicated member of the Savage Club. There he attended dinners and meetings for several decades, almost a piece of the furniture, some might have said. Then he died there, collapsing during a dinner. Such dedication was not uncommon.

The gentlemen's clubs entered our imagination at a deeper level too – in the guise of 221b Baker Street. What is the snug lounge and adjoining workroom of that den if not a version of a club? Mrs Hudson caters for the gentlemen's needs and they live at leisure, with plenty of time for the sleuths, Holmes and Watson, to go in pursuit of villains. That upstairs room has seeped into popular culture: a den of men of letters, a male province, and a sacrosanct adult's playroom where a schoolboy's dream of scientific gadgets and invitations to adventure fill the lives of two men at their ease in a protected world, somehow outside time, as all good fiction should be.

Harry was a member of the Crimes Club. He knew Harry Brodribb Irving, son of the great actor Sir Henry Irving, and he was also a friend of the journalist, playwright and novelist, George R. Sims. These two men were both members of this club. Harry explains the group and his involvement in their activities, in *My Notebook at Home and Abroad*:

> Although I knew H.B. Irving less intimately than Tree [Henry Beerbohm Tree, actor/producer] I saw more of him, for we not only met at the Garrick Club, but we were drawn together by a mutual interest in anything pertaining to crime and criminals. … There was (and I believe still is) a dining club called 'Our Society' … for the special purpose of bringing together those interested in such matters, and Irving and I were elected as members.

Harry explains a typical evening, and then goes on to make the point that these were not at all gloomy sessions, but in fact they were 'cheery' and he met men from all kinds of background, including Weedon Grossmith, the actor, painter and brother of George, the great Gilbert and Sullivan star and author with Weedon of the classic, *The Diary of a Nobody*, as noted earlier. In Harry's comments on him, we have a glimpse into the workings of the networking in this world that sustained Harry and his ilk in the ranks of the gentlemen clubmen:

> Weedon Grossmith would also occasionally look in at the Crimes Club, and I was much impressed by his modesty, not to say shyness, when we were first introduced, notwithstanding his great reputation as an actor and a playwright. Weedon had a passion for exploration, and introduced me as a character in one of his plays: *Billy's Bargain*, for which, (as we were then personally unacquainted) the writer apologized, although this was quite unnecessary.

They were a fair proportion of the literary, artistic and legal elite of their generation: they had excelled in the professional worlds of authorship, commerce, the bar and the higher journalism; they loved to meet in convivial and relaxed clubs, and they enjoyed parading their conversational talents in front of gaggles of like-minded men, perhaps at ease with brandy and a cigar, or sometimes giving a learned and entertaining talk about a topic of general interest. Peter Costello, in his book *Conan Doyle: Detective*, wrote that 'The members were ... so many students of contemporary crime. But they kept their affairs secret, so that even today ... little has been divulged about them. The club still exists and remains, as ever, exclusively secret.'

They were at first named 'Our Society' but later became the Crimes Club. They first assembled at the Great Central Hotel in London on 17 July 1904, after being discussed informally at the home of H.B. Irving, the year before. This was followed by a dinner at the Carlton Club in December 1903, and from that it is certain that the more formal conditions and guidelines for activities were formed.

Although members wanted the club to remain easy and chummy, with chats about fascinating criminal memorabilia or talks on infamous cases by professional members who were in the legal profession, word got around, and others wanted to join in.

They were an assortment of mainly university men, many from Oxford, where they had learned the importance of networking, but back then, the word used for that was simply *society*. They had all acquired the gentlemanly accomplishments expected of men of letters who wanted to stay in favour among their peers in the publishing world of the time. Most of them could hardly be called, in the parlance of the twenty-first century, movers and shakers. No, they had merely a common interest and they saw the benefits of sharing knowledge and experience.

The meetings soon attracted all kinds of members, and in 1909, one of the original members, Ingleby Oddie, resigned; he was miffed at the new identity of the club – something more streamlined and rather academic than at first conceived. The other founding members were, from the more celebrated persons: Sir Arthur Conan Doyle, Churton Collins, James Beresford Atlay, Lord Albert Edward Godolphin Osborne, George R. Sims, Max Pemberton, Fletcher Robinson, Harry Irving, C.A. (Lord) Pearson and A.E.W. Mason, and from the less well known, there were Arthur Lambton and a medical man from Norwich, Dr Herbert Crosse. Harry's criminological interests, and his unusual experience in that field, made him a valuable member.

There were many other personalities on the fringe of the club, also with profound interests in matters legal and criminal. There was George Ives, who started a vast collection of press cuttings in 1892, and his archive of such material was destined to run to 6,000 pages after sixty years of collecting. Many of his cuttings concerned criminal matters, and as his editor, Jeremy Brooks, noted in an anthology taken from the Ives cuttings, the man hated injustice. He wrote books on penal reform, too. Ives never joined the Crimes Club, but he did join Conan Doyle in another club: the Authors' Cricket Club, along with J.M. Barrie and P.G. Wodehouse. Here is yet another example of Conan Doyle being gregarious in a world of clubs and societies. He was always, since the time of his first real successes in literature, eager to be seen in society, and to mix with his peers.

In some ways, in its first identity, as Arthur Lambton wanted it, the Crimes Club was as much a source of play and relaxation as the charity cricket matches many of them played. Conan Doyle had even bowled out the great W.G. Grace. Conan Doyle and Alf Mason put on their whites alongside stars of the music hall and the theatre. That was the spirit of the club in 1903. But it was soon to transform itself into yet another exclusive group with an interest in a very topical theme – the nature of the criminal and the challenge of understanding the nature of the most heinous or the most astounding crimes.

The members typified the authors of their generation: creative minds coming into full powers of narrative and commercial know-how in an age of vast expansion in their readership. The 1890s had brought them new possibilities and new markets, as the popular journalism encouraged by George Newnes and Alfred Harmsworth expanded. One of the club members, Arthur Pearson, was of that breed, with his magazine *Pearson's Weekly*. Matthew Arnold referred to this popular writing with a strong literary impulse mixed together with informative, didactic work, as 'the new journalism'. With this came the rise of literary agencies (the first had appeared in 1875 with A.P. Watt) and the arrival of net book agreements for retail. The profession also had the Society of Authors, which began to organize advice, legal help and dissemination of information. In short, being a writer was, at the turn of the nineteenth century, becoming more of a career choice, although it was tough on those, such as George Gissing, who insisted on literary standards related to classic literature. For men like Conan Doyle and George Sims, the opportunities widened, such was the demand for popular storytelling. In that literary climate, the notions of brotherhoods of writers were extensions of professional attitudes. The working lives of writers became topics of intense interest, so much so that *The Idler* magazine ran a long series of interview pieces with the title 'Lions in their Dens'.

Were they a clique – in an age of cliques? That is, did they preserve their difference by being notably insular and exclusive? G.K. Chesterton saw a clique as a group with 'a tendency not only to talk shop, but to talk workshop. Like talkative art students, they show each other their work before it is finished; and like lazy art students, they often find this an excellent excuse for not finishing it at all.' Well, no, the members tended to see their projects through.

The years around 1900 were a time when writers generally took a very profound interest in crime and law in all its manifestations. Arnold Bennett, always keen to learn material for his craft, perhaps typifies this. In 1899 he sat on a coroner's jury at Fulham and heard four cases. He reflected in his journal on something that was always centrally important in the crime writers around Conan Doyle: 'The dramatic quality of sober fact. In two instances, the deceased persons had died from causes absolutely unconnected with the superficial symptoms. Thus a woman who had brought on a miscarriage and died, had died from heart disease.' In that brief note, Bennett encapsulates the allure of crime and transgression for the writer: the crime story has muddled interpretations and a variety of sources behind the act itself. The Crimes Club met in order to enjoy and to maximize that delight in digging for cause and effect in the confusion and mystery of human actions.

The first Crimes Club members were out to celebrate amateur sleuthing but it was far more than fun and relaxation: they enjoyed analysing cases, but even more challenging and absorbing was the enquiry into unsolved crimes and into the mysteries of motivation in criminal matters. The meetings were initially intended to be the kind of occasions in which professional men put their feet up, and over a brandy and a cigar, discuss a transgression and all its human complexity. Before the real professionalization of the social and psychological sciences, they explored deviant behaviour. In the infancy of criminology, they went deeply into the social and relational contexts of celebrated crimes, at a time when the police had only just begun to question the validity of the influential work of Cesare Lombroso. His notions of physiognomy as guides to criminal types had been accepted my many for some time, since the publication of his *L'Uomo Delinquente* in 1889 – although to be fair to the man, he did take an interest in a range of subjects related to criminal behaviour.

135

Harry writes about the club in *My Notebook at Home and Abroad*. Of his friend George R. Sims (known by all London as the columnist Dagonet), Harry recalls that he was a devoted student of crime. Harry went to see Sims, 'to inspect any new addition to his Black Museum, probably the most unique collection of criminal souvenirs in existence, to which I contributed a letter from Monsieur Deibler inviting me to see an execution.'

There were dozens of societies of this nature, and often one reads reports of meetings and finds the same names attending a good proportion of the clubs. If someone wished to start a Dickens Club, then most of the prominent writers around London would leap at the chance of being a member. A sport or passion for some activity relating to a man's manly pursuits might bring kindred souls together; cricket was a fine example of this, the sporty and clubbish aspects of such matters being seen in J.M. Barrie's team of writers and artists, the Allahakkbarries. Here, such luminaries as Conan Doyle, A.E.W. Mason and E.V. Lucas would play a friendly match on a village green in Sussex with an XI often enhanced by the presence of W.G. Grace or some other celebrity.

The clubs of these decades tell us a great deal about business as well. As with Corney Grain, the club was very much the inheritor of the old Georgian coffee house in terms of its importance as a place for wheelers and dealers. If a young, aspiring writer wanted the right contacts, then being a club member was the best possible move for networking. One contact led to another, of course, and eventually the new arrival would be seated next to someone like George Newnes, who owned papers and periodicals, or even (as was always possible) the Poet Laureate or the owner of the Gaiety Theatre might be sat next to you for that very long dinner.

Harry mixed with people from across the spectrum of the arts as well. For instance, one of his friends was the military painter, Richard Caton Woodville. There was in Harry a constant curiosity, a deep involvement in life and a profound interest in people. He encouraged others in their work, and in the arts in particular, he relished some kind of link in his networking and friendships to these other microcosms in which other practitioners worked. In 1900, for instance, he was keen to buy an engraving from Woodville, writing to him from the Junior United Services Club:

> My Dear Caton,
> I was so disappointed not to be able to come last night to Carlton, but my missus was so ill I really could not leave her. Please do not forget that you have promised an engraving of one of your pictures. Any one I shall prize as it deserves – I don't like to come bothering you at your studio, knowing how busy you are, but if the picture were sent to Claridge's Hotel, Brook St by any chance, I should get it safely!!! If it does not arrive I shall drop upon you one of these afternoons *chez vous*. *Nolens volens*.
>
> Harry de Windt

Some of his friends were very close indeed, and he had a great deal to say about these select comrades of club and foreign travel. A notable example was Haddon Chambers. He was a dramatist, born in Australia, who moved to England in 1882, and started to make his way writing stories and then dramatic works. He wrote short curtain-raisers at first, but in his play *Captain Swift* he really made an impact. This was followed by several other plays, and *The Idler*, performed in 1890, did very well. In his personal life, he was for a time the lover of the great operatic soprano, Dame Nellie Melba.

Harry wrote that Haddon was 'one of the closest friends' he ever possessed, and he adds, 'I have often sat with my old friend at his club, well into the small hours, listening, spellbound, to adventures in the Bush where he narrowly escaped death from hunger and thirst.' He met Haddon first in Paris, where Harry did so much of his socializing; Haddon was at the time in the flush of success after the production of his *Tyranny of Tears*. As *My Notebook at Home and Abroad* is packed with accounts of various friendships, the reader is struck by the number of important but short-lived ones. Yet in the case of Haddon Chambers, what Harry says about his friend is a clue to what he really valued in life. He wrote: 'Much of Haddon Chambers's worldwide social success was due to his marvellous knowledge of human nature, of which he made a careful study in every class of life.' But there was also in Harry, throughout his life, a need to play the fool, to recapture the mad and playful days of his time as a student at Magdalene College. Haddon appealed to that in Harry.

Harry recalls one of these memorable times in which Haddon's lighter side came through, when he talks about their time together in Paris: 'Haddon's face, at such times, would brighten, and the old mischievous twinkle come into his eyes, as when one evening he was addressed by a stranger as Lord Beatty (to whom he bore a striking resemblance).'

Harry even recalled their last meeting, which was at a public dinner in Paris, and Harry included a sketch in *My Notebook at Home and Abroad* that is a drawing and a note from Haddon on that occasion. Haddon died suddenly at his club after returning to London, on 28 March 1921. The note he left for Harry has a fragment of humour that was something of an in-joke between the two of them, and a humorous drawing of a certain 'Father Clement' whom they both knew.

In total contrast, there was one literary friendship that was undesirable; that of Horatio Bottomley. Here was a man who saw that exploitation of the greedy and gullible was the way to wealth and a life of ease. He soon understood, back in the late Victorian times when financial speculation was something of a fever among the lower middle class and indeed with the new rich, who loved speculation in company shares, that one might start a firm, issue and sell shares, and then sell lots of other shares, bearing the same number as initial certificates, because the majority of buyers would never find out what their investment did. The few who pestered and wrote letters would be fobbed off.

This strategy had a further level of iniquity: when investors became troublesome, he simply used his business-speak falsehoods and bluffs to increase their commitment to the cause by buying into supposed newly formed companies.

Now, this sort of white-collar crime can only be effected by the use of a certain marketing strategy that might be called 'Names dazzlement'. This is the kind of ruse used to impress investors by having lots of names attached to share information. Horatio knew that if he could attract and cajole famous people, respected in the City, to be involved in his schemes, then the little man would follow, thoughtlessly. The only other component needed for these schemes to work was that of mass communication: he needed a vast number of people to know about the plans and share sales. For this reason he started in the printing business. In the 1890s he had established himself in these nefarious schemes by starting the Hansard Union, whereby he made an amalgamation of printers and journalists, realizing that buying up small firms and gathering an alliance so that there could be lateral production was a way to impress the big names in the field.

He was in court in 1893, conducting his own defence, as he was to do throughout a long career of litigation, both defending and prosecuting. He had learned the rudiments of the law as it worked in the civil courts by working for a while in a clerical capacity in the legal profession. Now he was making his first appearance charged with fraud, and he came through well, being cleared. Not only was he exonerated, he also impressed some men high in the judiciary, and within a few years he was rubbing shoulders with High Court judges and famous barristers.

Bottomley was born in 1860 in Hackney Road, and was orphaned when very young. He was taken to Josiah Mason's orphanage in Birmingham, being helped to a certain extent by George Holyoake, a leading secularist of the time. Bottomley was strongly influenced by secularism and by the charismatic Charles Bradlaugh in particular. In fact, he always insisted that Bradlaugh was his real father, and kept a bust of that man in his office later in life.

In the early years of the twentieth century, Bottomley was established as a playboy, wealthy and enterprising, as well as a man of business. His superficial charm won him many friends, and he seemed to emulate the mythic John Bull – being a true Brit sportsman and 'character'. He was known through his successful newspapers, mainly *The Sun* and *John Bull*. His newspapers were channels for his own brand of cheery patriotism and Little Englander domestic values.

He liked nothing better than coming up with a competition, a challenge that would draw a few pounds out of each naïve reader who relished the conservative, middle-of-the-ground homely philosophy. *The Sun* was Bottomley's ideal mouthpiece for his obsession with a love of England, which was no more than a saleable veneer of traditional family values and imperial pride. He saw himself as the best potential prime minister the country had, and his newspapers were organs to disseminate his values and his aspirations for some ideal 'Britain' that existed only in his mind.

He owned racehorses, stayed in expensive hotels abroad, and most dear to his heart, he bought and developed his own country house, The Dicker, in Sussex. He also bought property in Pall Mall. On the profits of his chicanery, he gambled, kept mistresses and entertained grandly.

Around him he sensibly created a 'firm' so cleverly organized that he could wriggle out of any awkward situation, such as the frequent occurrence of disgruntled creditors or investors knocking on his door. At business premises, he had a front office, protecting him from the street and from unwanted callers; at the back of the property he had an escape route.

His aims were not simply in business. He had a lust for political power, and ran for Parliament, eventually succeeding in becoming Liberal MP for South Hackney in 1910. But a few years later he was bankrupt – and in the values of 2016, he was in debt to the tune of £6 million. But such was his resilience that he saw the arrival of the Great War as an opportunity to be both patriotic and criminal on a truly grand scale. He saw the possibility of massive profits in selling Victory Bonds at £1. The old methods were applied again: collect the money from the gullible masses and spend it. He saw that if a winner was given a sum of money and then the fact was made into a major story, the money from the gamblers would still keep coming.

But along the way, he made enemies, and one in particular – a man called Reuben Bigland, whom he had rejected as a partner in crime – was determined to see his enemy go down. He produced huge quantities of a pamphlet exposing Bottomley's fraud in the Victory Bonds. Here was a massive fraud waiting to be shot down in ignominy.

After all, Bottomley had become a public speaker commanding a large fee, a national personality and someone who even had the effrontery to advise the government and write to Lloyd George asking for a job on a national level, in what now would be called PR activity.

Harry met Bottomley and understood the fatal charm of the man. He met him during the Great War, and in his notebooks, Harry couldn't resist a compliment, in spite of the fact that he was writing about a known rogue: 'Whatever his subsequent misdeeds, I have never met a more talented and charming companion, and could, upon this occasion [dining with Bottomley] have filled a small notebook with the witty and original remarks which kept us convulsed with laughter.'

The fact that Harry had met Bottomley at the Café Royal says a great deal about Bottomley's success, and his ability to network, entertain and cajole those in his milieu. But in fact, Bottomley tried his trickery on Harry. He was accustomed to making friends and then pulling the new acquaintances into investing in his schemes. He offered Harry £100 as an inducement to invest in a South African venture. Harry took some time to deliberate, and then said no. That was the moment of insight as far as Harry was concerned:

> And this refusal seemed to cause my companion such surprise and annoyance, that he gave vent to a display of temper strangely at variance with his usual genial demeanour. ... 'I always thought you were a clever man!' was the financier's parting shot, when seeing that further persuasion was useless.

Harry, as a man who had appealed for investors in his Klondike scheme, would have understood where Bottomley was coming from in that interchange, but leaving the company – and the influence – of that rogue, was one of Harry's better decisions.

What we might conclude from this is that club life was, as well being all the other things discussed above, an adventure. A man might meet anyone in those rooms and bars, from a future contact in business to a complete charlatan: this was exactly the creative mix that Harry de Windt longed for, when the waiting and the restlessness kicked in.

Chapter 9

Camp Commandant and
Other Enterprises

*If a man be gracious and courteous to strangers, it shows
he is a citizen of the world.*

Francis Bacon, Essays

It might seem at this stage in Harry's life as though he never stood still
and that after each journey he planned the next while enjoying a drink
and a smoke in the Savage Club. But the truth is that in the Edwardian
years, although he did a major European journey, he found or made
the time to cultivate his other interests. He had the remarkable ability
to mix with a number of social groups in which particular vogues or
enthusiasm were being enjoyed, from paranormal trails to riding
horses. After dealing with his European journey and his war work,
these will be explained.

The first years of the new century, before the Armageddon of the
Great War, were dominated by Harry's journey into the Balkans,
recounted in his book *Through Savage Europe*, but he was busy with
a number of other things in those years. One highlight was the interest
he took in the latest technical obsession of gentlemen – adventure
flying. In 1909, Doncaster took centre stage in this area of sport and
technology as the town hosted the first aviation meeting in Great
Britain, using the expanse of the famous racecourse, home of the
classic St Leger.

Most of the celebrity flying aces and adventurers of the day were
invited, including the French contingent, led by Roger Sommer and
Léon Delagrange. Also appearing was the flamboyant Samuel F. Cody,
showman and brother of the famous Buffalo Bill Cody. He had taken

up flying during the period when his Wild West show was in Britain, and he clearly had a flair for the business. He met with the other international aviators for most of the month of October, and Harry was one of the stewards at the meeting.

In Harry's recollection, the affair was a 'fiasco' and he notes that the weather was dismal, but that seems to be a grumpy point of view. Later writers on the air show describe it as being quite sensational. Every flyer was paid the huge sum of £200 for taking part, and the real entertainers in the ranks of the competitors surely made those weeks memorable. Harry recalled Cody vividly: 'One day, however, the late Captain Cody [he was killed while flying in 1913] valiantly braved a scarcely perceptible breeze, and rose amidst deafening cheers, in a cumbersome plane which rattled like a threshing machine, to proceed a short distance about 60 feet high, and then fall heavily to the ground.'

He also recalls some trouble at that event, explaining that a Yorkshire crowd in the shilling stands rioted and tore down the railings. He claimed that 'they swarmed on to the course, intent upon mobbing everyone concerned with the venture, until dispersed by a strong force of police.' Harry was negatively selective on this experience: he does not mention the fact that Delagrange, flying his Blériot monoplane, won the Inauguration Cup and he exceeded the world airspeed record, reaching over 53 mph in front of the Doncaster crowd.

The Doncaster event was very successful, and the next year, women aviators were very much in the limelight: Hélène Dutrieu starred then, as she had proved her mettle by flying from Ostend to Bruges. In Doncaster, three male and three female pilots engaged in some good-humoured competition, and Hélène was in that entertainment.

A fellow steward at the 1909 air show was a friend of Harry's – fellow writer William Le Queux. In fact, Le Queux had planned a trek with Harry, a journey from Lapland to the Kola Peninsula, in the far north-west of Russia. In the end, they went to Lapland, but ventured no further. The fact is that Harry was too ill. He had had an operation,

though exactly what the illness was has not been ascertained. The press
reported that Harry had been given a 'medical order' to cancel the trip.
This was the cue for Le Queux to write a gentle satire, published in
Punch, which included the lines:

> *They dyed their moustaches a terrible tindt,*
> *Did Harry Le Queux and William de Windt.*
> *And they padded their waistcoats with bullet-proof lindt,*
> *Did Harry Le Queux and William de Windt.*
> *Now they've gone to the Arctic together: Hurreux!*
> *For William de Windt and Harry Le Queux.*

Harry had known Le Queux in another context as well: they were both
members of an interesting outfit known as the Legion of Frontiersmen.
In 1904, a letter to the papers called for men of adventure and
experience to gather together as a special force of fighters and
auxiliaries to be a resource for Britain in emergencies; the appeal was
for women as well as men. The guiding spirit was Roger Pocock, a
man after Harry's own heart, who had fought in the Boer Wars and
had also been in the ranks of the Canadian Mounted Police.

Pocock had proved himself to be a suitable leader for such an
intrepid band, having accomplished such feats as riding unarmed from
Canada to Mexico to grasp the world record for long-distance horse
riding. He had also been to Russia, so again, he appealed to Harry as
a kindred spirit. He saw the need for men of his own calibre as a
national reserve, and this came at the time when there was an
atmosphere of 'spy fever' in the land, as it was known that Germany
was developing as a nation with a massive and threatening military
status.

Harry and Le Queux responded and joined the ranks, along with
other men of action such as Morley Roberts, Edgar Wallace and a
number of war correspondents. Behind all this was the sense of failure
after the huge loss of life fighting the Boers, whose ability as
sharpshooters and snipers had shocked and rocked the British Army.
Now here was a bunch of shooting men and hardy explorers who were

gathering to form an unofficial reserve army. It was a sign of the times.

In April 1906 *The Times* reported on the organization, and gave this staggering information:

> We are informed by the secretary of the Legion of Frontiersmen that the formation of the corps which is to be a civilian and self-supporting force, has long been approved by the Secretary of State for War and that 6,000 men with colonial, frontier and sea experience have applied for enrolment.

It appears from this that the Legion was more than a case of 'boys' toys' and dressing up for parades.

All kinds of celebrities showed a great interest, including Sir Arthur Conan Doyle (whom Harry knew as a fellow member of the Crimes Club). Conan Doyle wrote a long letter to *The Times* with a cunning plan of his own relating to the Legion and its potential uses. He suggested that 'a thousand motorists, the number of which I am sure could be trebled or quadrupled, should organize themselves on the first news of invasion, could instantly fill up their cars with picked riflemen ... and convey them, with a week's food ... to the danger points.' He then appealed, 'I should be much obliged if every motorist who reads of this scheme and approves of it would send a card to that effect to the secretary, League of Frontiersmen, 6, Adam Street, Adelphi.'

In January 1907, the Legion engaged in a colourful piece of promotional activity: they gave an assault-at-arms at Manchester on the evening of the 20th of that month. A reporter noted that 'an interesting feature of the programme were two despatch rides – one from Newcastle-on-Tyne and the other from Portsmouth.' We have no information regarding Harry's involvement in this.

Matters concerning the Legion were a little shaky by 1909, as the press reported that a patriotic fund was to be started by *The Times* in order to save the apparently failing organization of patriots. It was reported that Pocock had made a desperate appeal 'to get sums of money from a shilling upwards.' But this was a strange rumour, as the piece was followed by a statement that the Legion was in a 'flourishing condition'.

The whole subject of the Frontiersmen is entirely typical of that Edwardian age of paranoia, when the fear of German militarism and expansionist thinking even included a nagging thought that the highly financed German Baltic Fleet was growing apace and wanted to challenge British naval supremacy. It was a climate in which any number of amateur enthusiasts turned their thoughts and abilities to the safety of the homeland. After all, this was the time when the Committee for Home Defence was formed, linked with the same for Imperial Defence, and from these came the MI5 and MI6 branches. At the heart of the general apprehension was the thought of invasion, and hence the need for the Frontiersmen, along with the Territorials, the Rifle Volunteers, and even the Boy Scouts.

Harry was a member of the League, but chooses not to say much about it. One wonders how he could possibly have had time to be involved.

Looking at the kinds of events happening at the time, this climate of fear is not at all surprising; after all, the enemy was not restricted to Germany. In July 1904, as people enjoyed their holidays along the East Coast, a British vessel was seized by the Russian navy as a 'prize of war'. Robert Blatchford, writing in *The Clarion*, gave the warnings that everyone expected: 'There is no fleet in the North Sea. There is no naval base on the East Coast. There are no fortifications worth mentioning, and no large military garrisons.'

Maybe Conan Doyle had a point with his suggestion of a motorized defence force. This entire social context of amateur military men provides a valuable insight into those times, when brotherhood in arms took so many forms, from rifle clubs to Scouts. The devotees of the 'male adventure' fiction of the 1890s were absolutely at home in that milieu. It was perfect for Harry's temperament.

Just before the Great War, Harry had a jaunt into North Africa. He never favoured that region for a major journey: it was far too densely populated and the climate was not cold enough for his tastes, but his account of that trip, amongst the French army and the colonial subjects of Mother France, was an interesting one, showing a side of Harry that is not often seen in his writings – the man who enjoys a risk. Usually he delights in preparation and military competence. But here, he immersed himself in an antagonistic society, trusting to low-level protection at times. As Charles Emmerson, in his book telling the story of important places on the eve of the Great War, explained, 'Bar a small and easily suppressed rebellion in the north-western village of Marguerite in 1901, it was over forty years since there had been any serious uprising against the French presence in Algeria.' But, there was always the brooding fear of a possible insurrection by the fanatics who promulgated Islam.

Yet again, Harry ventured into a territory that had a potentially violent social eruption waiting to happen. He found himself on a provincial train heading out into the desert, as he wanted to have a taste of the Foreign Legion and of the less orderly element in Algerian life. He was not disappointed. This trip was on the Béni Ounif line, and it must have seemed to him that he was destined to freeze – even in a desert trip: 'We crawled through a wilderness of gigantic grey boulders, torn and rent as though by some cataclysm of nature, and looking, in the grey light of dawn, as cold and lifeless as a lunar landscape. It was now bitterly cold … and patches of snow appeared in clefts of rock.'

He was always at home on trains, and relished the stimulating mix of ample food, conversation and discomfort. On this train, for instance, lunch was served 'to passengers in pyjamas, while we were traversing an ocean of sand … as we crept southwards, each *gare* became a miniature fortress.'

What he wanted on this journey was a frisson of excitement from the presence of immediate danger. He had always been attracted to the wild history of the area, being born in France and having absorbed issues of French imperial culture from the time of his youth. In this Saharan trip he mentioned that he had known Isabelle Eberhardt, a woman very much a kindred spirit to him. Isabelle, as Harry wrote, 'contrived to serve for some years as a private in a regiment of Spahis

[French Algerian cavalry] without disclosing her sex.' She was born in Switzerland in 1877, and she developed a deep interest in Islam in her youth, going to North Africa in 1897, taking a new name of Si Mahmoud Saadi, where she worked for General Hubert Lyautey. She became a scholar and writer.

Her background was complex and fascinating; mother was a Russian Jew and her father was a Russian anarchist called Alexandre Trophimowsky. She married and had children, and at first lived in Geneva. In Africa she had friends who encouraged her writing in her new life in North Africa, where she married a Spahi called Ehnni. She was then involved with a publisher called Barruand, who sent her on a mission to act as a war correspondent, just after the Battle of El-Moungar. She was more than likely engaged in some kind of espionage also, and this was destined to be a horrendous assignment. She became very ill and stayed in a mud house at Aïn Séfra, where she died after a flood. Harry adds to that tale, 'Here this remarkable woman (with hundreds of other victims) perished, to be laid to rest, with military honours, in a little Moslem cemetery just outside the town, in the great lonely desert which, in life, had been her only home.'

Harry arrived at the garrison town of Béni Ounif and found this a place where 'vice stalked naked, and uncloaked by darkness' as he studied the prostitutes of the place, the dancers and ladies of the night, called 'Ouled Naïls' – and they were but one sign of a shady, perilous outpost. He wrote that he always walked with a revolver in his hand in the town, and took real care when he and a guide ventured deeper into the byways of the town, beyond the military presence:

> Here were a few shops in the shape of small dark recesses in the walls, where raw meat, vegetables, fruit, wearing apparel, old scrap-iron and all sorts of rubbish were exposed for sale; also native-made saddlery and Eastern weapons, which, mingled with modern rifles and Browning revolvers, showed that the Zenagans are not always peaceful agriculturalists. There may have been fifty or sixty people in that alley, all of whom turned away as we passed by, and these, and the elders,

were the only human beings we saw throughout that day, in a place containing 3,000 souls!

He then stayed some time with the French battalion, and, as Harry was always prying into punishment, ever since his first steps into studying prisons, he investigated the punishments inflicted on rebellious or criminal locals. The result was a series of notes on barbaric acts, such as the punishment known as the *crapaudine*: 'Here I found a prisoner lying sideways on the ground, clad only in vest and trousers, while nearer approach disclosed that the poor wretch's wrists and ankles were so tightly bound together that his body almost formed a circle.' The *crapaudine* was inflicted for two or three days, and Harry was fully aware of the awful illnesses that would result from this treatment.

He managed to put up with this depressing outpost of empire for three weeks, and then he was headed back north. But, in spite of the conditions, his verdict on the soldiers who held that border was very positive: 'The call of the Sahara is as resistless as that of the Arctic or Far East. And seldom have I witnessed, even in Africa,' and he 'waved goodbye to those brave fellows and the little white town.'

When the Great War came, at first Harry took up the post of a recruiting officer. Clearly, there were plenty of useful roles and responsibilities for men such as him. After all, he had military experience, and his time with the Legion of Frontiersmen had kept up his interest in weaponry; his pursuits in the world of turf had proved his horsemanship, and he certainly had leadership qualities. But what was to prove to be his main contribution to the war effort was his employment as a commandant at a prisoner of war camp for German military personnel. The question of prisoner of war camps for German captives and interns was to prove a very demanding enterprise for the authorities in both world wars, with a tendency for the War Office to create camps on a pragmatic basis, often very unsuccessfully. For instance, the camp at Swanwick, Derbyshire, in the Second World War, had its escapees, as did Grizedale Hall in Cumbria. Until solid camps were made on the Isle of Man, for instance, in the Great War, there were camps hurriedly prepared and poorly managed. Harry was not the man to do a second-rate job, and from the start he took a Prussian attitude to management.

This role was perfect for him really, though he considered it dull. He had proved, in his writings and in his expeditions, that he had a specialized knowledge of prisons and penology. Even after his work on Siberian prisons, he had made prison visits. In *True Tales of Travel and Adventure*, for instance, he wrote a piece on a visit to Wormwood Scrubs, and in *My Restless Life* he does the same for Aylesbury Prison. These two pieces – an essay and a memoir – show Harry at his best as a documentarian who mixed powerful and vivid autobiographical testimony with the necessary data for a genre of factual literature. He had the knack of selecting the most topical and contentious aspects of prison life; at Aylesbury, which was a woman's prison, for instance, he was reporting on a very new initiative. Special jails for women offenders, other than Holloway, had been few, and it was in the first decade of the twentieth century that such places were created outside London. He immediately brought the prison life into the reader's sharp consciousness when at Aylesbury, he reported, 'Take the daily diet, for instance: butcher's meat, coarse and greasy, four days in the week; on the others, canned food, watery soup and soft pudding. What a menu after the dainty, appetizing meals of upper social life!' Here he was thinking primarily of the notorious Florence Maybrick, condemned to die for the murder of her Liverpool husband, and then reprieved. She had been held at Aylesbury not long before his visit.

Still, in spite of Harry's conclusions after seeing Aylesbury that the experience of a British jail brings down health and character, he cannot help a comparison, as Paris is his spiritual home:

Nevertheless, as I drove away, and the bright lights of the prison faded in the dusk, another prison recurred to my mind – a certain foul dungeon in Paris, where innocent women are herded with the vilest of their sex, and where vice and disease stalk rampant. And I felt glad that, although strict discipline prevails at Aylesbury, it is maintained in a humane, unobtrusive manner, which must to a great extent mitigate the horrors of penal servitude.

He was thinking of the Saint-Lazare prison and hospital in Paris, which he had also visited. His verdict on that was that the penal sections were 'fruitful breeding places of crime' but that the hospital was a 'redeeming feature'.

In terms of Britain, where he was now to have the chance to manage a prison himself, he had a sound knowledge of Wormwood Scrubs, so he had an idea about the British mindset in running such places, compared to that he had found in Russia. In his chapter 'A Day at Wormwood Scrubs' in *True Tales of Travel and Adventure*, Harry is visiting when the jail is merely twenty years old; it was peculiar in that it was built buy convict labour.

In his book *Legal London* (1999), Mark Herber pointed out that at that time Wormwood Scrubs, with a population of about a thousand, was the largest prison in Britain. Today, it is still high on the list, along with Wandsworth and Lindholme, in terms of notional operational capacity. They all top the thousand mark, with the Scrubs being about 1,400. But of course we now live in an era in which 'Titan prisons' and 'Superjails' are planned and discussed, as size and scale appear to many to be the answer to our prison problems. But there are dissenting voices. Big is not necessarily beautiful in terms of size. The prison administrator's dream, summed up in the phrase 'happiness is closed doors and no bells ringing', is surely related to the size of the prison population.

It was just the same c. 1900. Images of the Scrubs show either a massive, factory-like side perspective or the impressive entrance, evoking a medieval castle. This edifice has a distinctive patterned stone appearance that from a distance looks like a cluster of white Roman numerals on the two towers, and a Norman arch at the centre. It was built purposefully to suggest the same kind of doom-laden thoughts as were Dante's lines on Hell: 'Abandon all hope, ye who enter here.'

The first steps towards constructing Wormwood Scrubs and

slotting it neatly into the national prison system were taken in 1874, when it was no more than a shed for the warders and a corrugated iron building for the inmates. In fact, the fine old tradition of having prisoners involved in the construction of prison buildings (and indeed in the business of the hangman) applied here: a group of prisoners, immediately after their sentences ended, were employed to enlarge the establishment. When, a year later, work had progressed so that a proper brick prison was envisaged, the place was in step with the greatest innovation in the British penal system – nationalization and the streamlining of the whole network of prisons across the land.

We have a good idea of what the prison looked like in its first years, because Arthur Griffiths, a prominent writer on prison life, was working at the Scrubs in the 1870s, and in his book *Secrets of the Prison-House* (1894) he provides a drawing, made in 1874, showing a very long block with an entrance and gatehouse in the centre, and another parallel smaller block. All around is a wasteland, bare of all growth except a few tree stumps, and there are pools of no doubt brackish water around the landscape.

Griffiths also provides his own take on the prison as it was in its incomplete stage:

> This, perhaps the finest of modern prisons, of the most vast dimensions, and the most perfectly appropriate architecture, was then in process of construction. It was an interesting scene: the busiest activity prevailed everywhere. Some were digging the foundations of a new block of buildings; others in regular procession were wheeling in and depositing barrows full of newly prepared concrete; others more distant were engaged in the multifarious business of brick-making.

The brick-making involved machines, producing moist bricks, which were then taken to large stacks where they were 'skintled' – trimmed – and then dried.

Harry was there when all this was new, and the fresh, radical new organization of the prison system was just beginning to set in after teething troubles. He is generally impressed: 'Indoors there is more life and animation, and the prison conveys a general impression of light, and activity not inconsistent with absolute cheerfulness.' There is meaningful work being done; trades are being taught, and when he asks about the treadmill, that giant wheel that had been used throughout the century to provide prisoners with tough work to drive a wheel much like a mill wheel in production of commodities, he is told that it has gone. He also sees 'all creeds represented' in the places allocated for prayer and worship; the one blot on the landscape is the use of solitary confinement. He concludes, 'That Wormwood Scrubs is a model establishment of its kind no one can deny; but if confinement in a luxurious sick room soon becomes irksome, what sufferings may not underlie even a month of penal seclusion.'

He was now to be tested, given a position of power in a prison. Harry de Windt, in 1915, was transmuted from commentator on jails to commandant of a jail. The internment of Germans – both combatants from the front and internment of Germans at home in Britain – was in full swing, and it was chaotic and piecemeal, to say the least. There were camps for internment scattered everywhere in Britain, and many of these were transient, put together *ad hoc* simply because there were so many people to gather together and surround with barbed wire.

The situation regarding German prisoners was pragmatic: camps were hurriedly made and various reserve military personnel brought in to act as guards. In Wales, for instance, where Irish Sinn Féiners were interned after the 1916 Easter Rising, a bantam regiment was brought in to guard the prisoners. At other times, older men, with army experience, were drafted in. This all depended on the state of the theatre of war over in France or Flanders. Basically, the men given the task of running the camps had to be prepared for any kind of rapid reshufflings and changes in administration. Harry was nothing if not adaptable.

Looking back with the wisdom of hindsight, and from very different humane values, today's readers looking at internment in the Great War will be astounded at conditions, and indeed at the very basis of it, which was rooted in fear and paranoia. Naturalized Germans were shunted to camps; talented artists and musicians were bundled into camps with dangerous types with revolution in their minds, and sometimes whole communities were dragged away to be settled in strange, isolated spots across the United Kingdom. As for the military prisoners, they had camps of their own at some points, but then, as the war went on, they were mixed with civilian internees. In this chaotic situation, Harry became the manager of a camp known as Black Park, in Buckinghamshire. When war broke out, he had been stranded in France, and had recently travelled across Europe, so he had seen, and been amongst, German officers on that trek. He had not formed a good opinion of them at all, and he had previously had some unpleasant experiences in Berlin. Now here he was, in a position of power over hundreds of captured German soldiers, and in the middle of the rural beauty of the South of England.

It was a sharp contrast to his first wartime post of Recruiting Officer in Hampstead – work that he described as 'intolerably irksome'. Black Park had earlier been used as a forestry camp, run by Canadians; the business had been to produce timber, which was needed in vast quantities for making entrenchments and coverings in the theatre of war in France and Belgium.

Harry was wise enough to see that discipline must be established at the very outset. One of the puzzling features of prison establishments is that the few command and control the many, and that a massive prison population submits, most of the time, to discipline. Five hundred prisoners could soon overpower and master a guarding force of, say, thirty men. But if the thirty men have not only weapons, but are part of a palpably potent regime that is enforced by force of character as well as *force majeure*, then the regime works, with a social stratification like a factory or a regiment. All this meant that power had to be exercised at the beginning. Harry explained in *My Notebook at Home and Abroad*:

> Most of these men were Saxons and Bavarians who tried it on
> by refusing to go out to work on the first morning that I

assumed command. They were therefore formed up in square in the prison yard, where, with a revolver in one hand and a watch in the other, I informed them that unless they were at work in the woods within five minutes I would shoot their Feldwebels [sergeants who maintained order] and try everyone else by court martial. And they went like lambs!

It would not be difficult to portray Commandant de Windt as a complete martinet. When one of his charges wrote home, his letter included a character assessment of Harry: 'This place is Hell, and the Commandant is well suited to it for he is a thin, dark little man, with a face like a devil!' In truth, Harry's opinion on running a prison was one of absolute iron control: his attitude is summed up with his general statement that he could never understand why the War Office 'showed such consideration towards the soldiers of a nation which was daily subjecting our own prisoners to mental and physical torture.' He did, it must be admitted, encounter some repulsive behaviour, such as the eating of a little dog by one group of Germans. But he had no real respect for the League of Nations, which was charged with inspections and dealing with complaints – just as, for instance, the American Ambassador was doing for British prisoners in Germany. One day he tapped a man on the arm for disobeying an order, and two men from the Swiss Legation came to interrogate him.

He also experienced one of the main concerns of any prison manager – the reception and dissemination of information by inmates. The ways of prisoners in wartime are devious and inventive in the extreme, as we know from Colditz stories and the film *The Great Escape*, and Harry experienced this for himself:

One contrivance ... was a substance which, resembling twine, was used to secure parcels etc., received by the prisoners, who always begged to be allowed to retain what appeared to be ordinary string. One day, however, my interpreter discovered that the latter was tightly rolled-up paper, which, when opened, disclosed minutely written but quite legible instructions regarding a proposed aerial raid on the South Coast of England.

Harry did have some notable guests to break the monotony of the work. One member of the Royal Family came – a princess who was not named – and also the stage and early silent film actor Charles Hawtrey (1858–1923), who was a massive star in 1915. Hawtrey was knighted after the war, and certainly his reputation was very high when he paid the surprise visit to Black Camp. The doyen of theatre history in the mid-twentieth century, W.J. MacQueen-Pope, wrote that Hawtrey was 'the consummate actor of his day. ... There has never been anyone to eclipse him in his own style.' As far as Harry was concerned, the visit led to some humour, as an inmate recognized the star, pointing out that he had been a waiter at the Savoy before the war and had often served the great actor then.

It is hard to explain what might have been the ideal person to manage a camp like this; in the Second World War, one writer visited such a camp, and he met a colonel who was doing the same work as Harry had done. He offers a profile of the ideal type for the work:

The Colonel had been through the last war, and was on the reserve list when called up to organize the 'hotel'. He is the ideal man for the job: a bachelor who likes living in the depth of the country, a humorous, humane disciplinarian, who is resolved to make his captives as comfortable as regulations allow.

That could be Harry, although 'bachelor' is hardly applicable.

There were wider issues also that affected his work. When he took over command at Black Park, it was in a nationwide fervour of anti-German riots and prejudice, notably after the sinking of the ship *Lusitania* off Ireland in May 1915 by a German torpedo boat. This prompted headlines such as this from *The Weekly Dispatch*: 'How many Germans are living in this country and are not in gaol?' As Robert Winder explains, in his book on immigration to Britain:

Trouble was stacked like tinder throughout the country ready to be ignited by anything from a perceived failure to show enough respect to the Union Flag to an impatience with the speed of service in the bread queue. At Deptford, a German shop in the High Street had bricks hurled through the window. Soon there was a crowd of 5,000 or so throwing stones and setting fires.

Harry was well aware that his task was a delicate one, and he thought like a European as well as an Englishman. That duality of outlook gave him the ability to handle people and situations with a clear objectivity, and that was a valuable asset in this particular post.

As for the Black Park camp, which was near Wexham in the south of the county, it is a countryside centre now, and memories of the German camp are barely even vestigial. The work Harry did there and the possibility of an oral history record has been entirely wiped out. His account of life there seems to be the only testimony to the community within the barbed wire, and that applies to so many internment camps from both world wars.

There is no doubt that Harry was no stranger to the law courts. In addition to his appearances regarding his failed marriage, he spent time in court with regard to criminal actions as well. Immediately post-war, after his spell as recruiting officer and prison commandant, Harry found himself enmeshed with his long-standing friend Lord Alfred Douglas, known as 'Bosie', who was involved in the notorious trial of his friend Oscar Wilde back at the end of the last century. Harry knew Wilde and Bosie through his mother's close friendship with Wilde's wife, Constance. On top of that, Harry had met Wilde at Oxford.

Subsequently, Harry and Bosie were friends, and when the latter found himself in legal trouble, Harry stood by him.

In 1919, Bosie, who was the younger brother of Percy, the then current Lord Queensbury, was running a magazine financed by his brother's rich friend, a certain James Conchie. This was *The Academy* at first, but then became *Plain English*, and was later to be renamed yet again as *Plain Words*. Bosie was undoubtedly a talented journalist and writer, but he had, for thirty years before the present editorship, been litigious in the extreme. There had been so many court cases in his life, conducted at the same time as he pursued his interests in the turf and a succession of business interests, that his biography today reads like that of a constantly paranoid man fleeing from trouble and stress. Of course, his tendency to hit back at any affront or insult created more legal problems for him, and in 1919 he went too far.

Around that time he was flitting from one interest and allegiance to another, and he happened to meet another editor from Belfast called Pim, the friendship leading Bosie to imagine he was sympathetic to the cause of Sinn Féin and thus also hating the English (he saw himself as a Scot – which he was). He changed his mind again when Sinn Féin appeared to indulge in acts of horrendous cruelty, but Bosie still needed an axe to grind, and he needed to stir up trouble. Unfortunately, this time he became obsessed, as many did at the time, with the rich Jews who had made their mark in British industry and commerce. Several successful Jewish entrepreneurs had bought massive homes in the classiest part of London, and had made their mark in political circles, so that Bosie, along with many others, considered that most of England's ills were down to their influence.

In 1923 he took *The Morning Post* to court for libel. In April 1922 it had printed this: 'It must no longer be a paying proposition for men like Mr Crosland and Lord Alfred Douglas to invent vile insults against the Jews.' The paper had a point. In Bosie's *Plain English*, there had been a campaign, described by H. Montgomery Hyde in his biography of Bosie: 'Thus *Plain English* attacked a "clique of rich Jews" such as Sir Alfred Mond and Sir Ernest Cassel, whose machinations in the City were allegedly responsible for the faults of international finance.'

But in the course of the case, which Bosie won but emerged with no honour, something else came out in the process of Bosie being examined by Patrick Hastings. Foolishly, Bosie had developed a strong opinion, based on accusations made by an ex-officer who had been certified insane, that the battle of Jutland of 1916, in which the German fleet defeated the British in terms of tactics, though not in the context of overall strategy in the North Sea, that Winston Churchill, former First Lord of the Admiralty, had been to blame. Even worse, Bosie believed that Churchill had been influenced by the Jewish men of power.

Hastings fastened on to this in court. This interchange took place:

HASTINGS: 'You say later on in reference to Mr Churchill: "It is true that by most subtle means and by never allowing him more than a pony ahead, this ambitious and brilliant man, short of money and eager for power, was trapped by the Jews. After the Jutland business, his house was furnished by Sir Ernest Cassel." Do you mean to say that Mr Churchill was financially indebted to the Jews?'

BOSIE: 'Yes, certainly.'

Bosie claimed that he had information that Churchill had been given £40,000 by Cassel after Jutland. In modern values that needs to be multiplied by about fifty. Now, Bosie added to this something more sensational: he thought that the Jews had also plotted to kill Lord Kitchener, who had drowned at sea aboard HMS *Hampshire* off Orkney in 1916. Bosie replied in court, giving his reasons for this belief: 'I had enough in my mind to convince me that Kitchener was murdered to prevent him from reaching Russia, because if he had arrived there, the revolution would not have taken place and the war would have been shortened by several years.'

Churchill, in the dock while Bosie had stormed out, having taken offence at Hastings' attack on these beliefs, explained why he had not taken action against Bosie on this matter before. He said that the Attorney General, Sir Douglas Hogg, had advised that it should be allowed to pass without response, as publicity for such a small and contemptible little paper would not help matters.

But Bosie pressed the self-destruct button. Yes, he won that case, but then, in August 1923, he spoke at a public meeting at the Memorial Hall in London, and there he repeated the allegations against Churchill. The result was a prosecution for libel. Churchill could not let this go without a response and a challenge. In December 1923, Bosie was in the dock at the Old Bailey, facing a libel charge. He pleaded not guilty, and was defended by Cecil Hayes, and Churchill was represented by Sir Douglas Hogg. The trial lasted four days, and one of the most damaging aspects for Bosie was that Harold Spencer, the officer who had given him information, was shown to be unreliable. He was reminded that his captaincy had been removed, as shown in *The Gazette*, and that he had been certified insane by a medical board. His facts were undermined also. He was reminded that he had said Churchill had met the witness at a flat owned by Lady Randolph Churchill, but as Hogg pointed out, 'Do you know that Lady Churchill never had a flat in London at all?'

Bosie had no chance of winning. Mr Justice Avory, before passing sentence, said that Bosie had been 'absolutely reckless in what he wrote and published'. He then added:

In view of your previous experience in this court it is obvious that you must be taught a lesson, and like other persons, suffer punishment. The sentence of this court is that you be imprisoned in the second division for six months, and at the expiration of that sentence find a surety in £100 to keep the peace and be of good behaviour.

Before the trial, there had been widespread fears about possible activities of German spies in Britain, and of the infiltration of powerful Germans in the very heart of government. Bosie was sure that the death of Kitchener was down to some machinations in which Churchill was involved. The basic fact was that the *Hampshire*, with Kitchener on board, had left Scotland without accompanying escorts of battleships. A committee of enquiry was formed, which included Harry, Lady Edith Fox-Pitt (Bosie's sister), General Prescott-Decie and the Hon Mrs Greville-Nugent.

These general fears and media panics were partly founded on influential reports. The *London Evening News*, for instance, expressed a common view: 'It is felt all over London that Lord Kitchener met his death through foul or treacherous spying.' Panikos Panayi, an expert on German internment during the Great War, adds another perspective: 'Horatio Bottomley [editor of *John Bull*, a patriotic paper] blamed the sinking of the *Hampshire* on both "official bungling", because the ship did not have sufficient escort, and upon the "sneaking, slimy Hun, who pollutes our atmosphere by his presence and defiles our streets by his very footsteps".'

At the same time there was a smear campaign against Sir Edgar Speyer, a magnate of German descent; in the diary of the Earl of Crawford, there is a reference that explains the feeling about Speyer at the time. He wrote that at a dinner in Downing Street, at which Churchill was in attendance, 'the actual position and disposition of the fleet was the subject of conversation.' Similarly, Lord Charles Beresford made a speech in which he blamed the sinking of three British cruisers in the North Sea on 'assassins in the shape of spies'.

It was in this atmosphere that Harry and friends attended the court to watch Bosie go down for libel – sentenced to the six months.

The 'divisions' referred to relate to the three divisions applied in a sentence of penal servitude with hard labour. Only prisoners in the first division could wear their own clothes and have food delivered from friends outside. In the second division, at least Bosie would have been given a mattress (unlike Harding, referred to in the introduction, who had a plank in his cell).

On 13 December 1923, Bosie was taken to the Scrubs. Oscar Wilde, Bosie's friend and lover, is arguably the most notorious literary prisoner in English literature, closely followed by John Bunyan. In his writing he had a lot to say about the prison regime in Britain at the end of the nineteenth century, and in his *Ballad of Reading Gaol*, he produced a classic of prison poetry. In an ironic echo of that experience, the man who had been deeply involved in Wilde's case, Bosie, walked into Wormwood Scrubs, a prisoner, in 1924.

In 1926, Harry was involved in the stormy life of Bosie yet again.

This time it did not involve appearances in court, but simply advice on Bosie's relationship with his son, Raymond, the fruit of Bosie's marriage to Olive Custance. Raymond was to become the unfortunate subject of an emotional tug of war between Olive's father and Bosie. In 1925–26, as letters show, Harry was called in to give advice when Raymond was associated with a Miss Lacey. Raymond thought that Harry was interfering, and should keep out of the family squabble. Bosie, it seemed, did not want Miss Lacy and his son to be married, and Harry, as the rather avuncular man of the world, should perhaps have kept out of it.

However, in early November 1923, Harry was in court – this time prosecuting *The Spectator* for libel. Harry had Cartwright Sharp, a very experienced barrister, acting for him with regard to an alleged libel concerning a review of Harry's book, *My Notebook at Home and Abroad*. In the law report pages of *The Times*, the issue was explained:

> Unfortunately, in criticising the book, statements were made which could easily be regarded as reflections on Mr de Windt himself. One passage which was complained of was this: 'He has been hard put to it to show that his comradeship with spies and swindlers was innocent.' The plaintiff had now been assured that neither the reviewer nor any person connected with *The Spectator* intended to attack him. It might be that the words were founded on a misconception of some of the innuendoes in the books.

Terms were arranged, and Harry received a sum in compensation. An apology had already been published, and the reviewer had written privately to apologize. But the fact was that parts of the book were quoted that were open to misinterpretation. None of the accused parties intended any sleight, but the journal had to pay up.

There was another side to Harry, rather opposed to the hard-headed man of action. He, along with so many literary men of his generation, had an abiding interest in the paranormal, and in other supposed 'fads' of his day such as fringe medicine and even in the province we associate today with such figures as Uri Geller, the illusionist spoon bender, and Derek Acorah, who describes himself as a spirit medium. What all this amounts to is the interesting passion he had for all things inexplicable or marginal. These interests ranged from paranormal experiments to the study of supposed significance of moles on the face and the body.

One insight into this is in his psychical activities. In Theodore Besterman's book on scrying, or crystal gazing, we have a memory of Harry being involved in an experiment. Besterman was a Polish scholar and researcher, born in 1904. He became an investigating officer for the Society for Psychical Research from 1927 to 1935, and later published widely on the subject. He also became an expert on the works of Voltaire. Harry figures in one of his popular works of psychic investigation, and he quotes a researcher called Myers, relating to an experiment linking raps to scrying. The theory in these areas of research presents the view that looking in a mirror may open up scenes from the past, or from the dead, or even show scenes or faces from elsewhere in the contemporary world. The latter seems to be the case with Harry's testimony. Myers wrote:

> In September 1892, on the occasion of the first meeting of Mr de Windt and Miss A. and Mrs A. (all present at the time), and a letter from Mr de Windt confirms two of the main points, the latter wrote the word Doishowalinksky, which at first was thought to be a sentence, but turned out to be a name well-known to Mr de Windt, and recognized by the latter … 'I can only tell you that I distinctly saw the face of an exile I am acquainted with, one Dombrowski, who is (or was) located at Tomsk. … a message was also sent to me …' It is not known whether Dombrowski is dead or alive.

Myers goes on to state that Harry also recognized another figure seen in a crystal, a 'stunted hillman who dyes his hair with red clay'. More mystery was to follow, this time involving Harry's sister, the Ranee of Sarawak:

A few days later a message was given by raps to Lady Brooke, 'Tell your brother that Shiskine is the man to help him.' Neither Miss A. nor Mr de Windt had ever consciously heard of Shiskine, but in the *St James Gazette* of 24 September they observed that M. Shiskine had received a certain high appointment, which explained the message.

Of course, we will never know Harry's reactions to all this, but we can glean from his other comments incorporated into his books that his sense of adventure was applied as much to the paranormal and inexplicable as it was to the trek to distant climes. This aspect of Harry may be seen in his memory of being in Paris, spending the evening at the famous cabaret run by the artist Aristide Bruant. He was with Alfred Capper, a man who made a showman's living as a thought-reader. Capper had a show that he presented everywhere on his world travels – a melange of dissolving knots and silk handkerchiefs, and Harry recalls that the audience were entranced. He explains, 'Capper's professional methods were rather startling to those not prepared for violent treatment; for having selected a subject, he would suddenly seize the latter by the wrist, and drag him at breakneck speed regardless of furniture, stairs or any other obstacle until he had attained his object.'

In Harry's reflections on Capper's belief in the personal 'aura' we have surely a glimpse into the traveller's rather easy acceptance of some of these occult topics. He reflects, 'Alfred taught me how to produce this phenomenon, by sitting in darkness, holding the fingers of each hand together, and very slowly parting and rejoining them until the strange light appeared, which, to my surprise, it did, as any reader can prove to his own satisfaction.'

In Paris, he also met Count Hamon, a performer known as 'Cheiro' in the world of entertainment. Here we find Harry making little distinction between the showman and the serious researcher, but at least he was willing to give these showmen a chance, be they charlatans or harmless conjurors. The account of Cheiro reveals that Harry was also an amateur palm reader, and he learned this from

'Count Hamon' – who was actually William Warner, born in Dublin in 1866. Warner had travelled out to Bombay, and there he acquired a Guru from whom he learned whatever it was that Europeans saw as his 'clairvoyant' skills, which were coupled with palmistry and astrology.

Harry tells us that he learned his skills from Hamon, and that in fact, although it is out of print, Harry himself published a book on palmistry. He explained, 'Cheiro achieved great fame in London as a reader of hands some years ago. This brilliant Irishman gave me many useful hints concerning palmistry, a science to which I have devoted many years of study.' It is interesting that Harry uses the word 'science' here. Many would doubt the suitability of that word. But certainly Hamon made an impact as a 'Society palmist' and consequently he mixed in celebrity circles. Another literary man, Mark Twain, wrote in Cheiro's visiting book, 'Cheiro has exposed my character to me with humiliating accuracy. I ought not to confess this accuracy, still I am moved to do so.' It also has to be noted here that one of his readings was for William Pirrie, the chairman of Harland and Wolf, who built the *Titanic*. In his autobiography, Cheiro explained that he predicted that Pirrie would soon be in great trouble, with his life under threat, and the narrative of the sinking of that massive ship was foreseen.

The list of Cheiro's meetings with celebrities is very impressive, including Oscar Wilde, Henry Stanley, Charles Parnell and Lillie Langtry. He even read the palm of King Edward VII.

Even more interesting, with regard to Harry's paranormal interests, is his passion for the subject of using moles as a means of divination. The name he uses for this is 'moleosophy'. He has given an explanation of the beginnings of this strange interest:

It may interest those interested in such matters to know that divination by means of the moles on the human countenance is almost as correct and reliable as that obtained by means of cheiroscopy [palmistry]. ... My attention was called to this fact by an ancient work by one Richard Saunders (published in London during the reign of Charles II) which I purchased one day at a bookstall on the Quai Voltaire, and which proved so engrossing that I rewrote the portion relating to moleosophy in modern and readable English.

The result was *Moles and Their Meaning*, published by C.A. Pearson, and that in itself is significant, because Pearson, the publisher, was himself very much involved in fringe medicine, most notably in treatments for impaired vision, as he himself was eventually to go blind. Pearson had also published, for instance, *Pearson's Dream Book* and *Hands and How to Read Them*.

The book by Richard Saunders was published in 1671, with the most unsnappy title of *Physiognomie and Chiromancie, Metroscopie, the Symmetrical Proportions and Signal Moles of the Body, Fully and Accurately Explained, with Their Natural Predictive Significations*. Harry definitely found a more appealing title. Saunders was very much the all-rounder in the mould of Renaissance Man, being a historian, astrologer and fringe medicine fanatic, and all these pursuits were covered by the blanket term of his era, 'Natural science'. He links moles with astrology, and takes as his source a Greek seer known as Melampus.

Harry was entranced by this. On the website Odd Books (see bibliography) Harry is put to the test. The writer there refers to a mole formerly on the cheek of the singer Enrique Iglesias, and then Harry is quoted. Harry's actual words are: 'Denotes misfortune, but only at an advanced age. Youth and middle age shall be peaceful and prosperous. This sign is especially favourable to the knowledge of secret and occult things – a marvellous and intuitive reader of human character.' The web writer comments, referring to Enrique as 'prosperous', that Harry is 'spot on'.

This is all very strange, and we have to ask what these hobbies show in Harry. Undoubtedly, we have the restless mind at work here. When there were no journeys on huge land masses, his mind had to engage with something that was equally indefinable and that presented some kind of challenge. He was equally at home being in the public sphere as a personality too, recommending health products. He was, for instance, featured in an advertising campaign by Sanatogen in 1911, when he was quoted alongside the strapline 'Promise me you will try Sanatogen for your nerves', and his quote was, 'I have derived enormous benefit from taking a short course of Sanatogen. Sanatogen in a few short weeks has made a new man of me, physically and mentally.' He also recommended some brands of chocolate (as did Captain Scott) and he was obviously following, or initiating, the great tradition of travellers and explorers obtaining provisions by means of helping with promotions of goods.

This is not to denigrate his motives though; he was equally active in the war years in raising funds, particularly for establishing such things as nursing homes and worthy causes. In 1911, for instance, he chaired a meeting at which Bishop Blair spoke, at her Majesty's Theatre, in order to raise funds for schools and nursing homes in the Falkland Islands.

By the post-war years, when Harry's contribution had been mainly in the work at the Black Camp, he was busy with occasional writing and with these recreations. With his very considerable circle of friends, he was never idle or bored. After the war, in addition to his fads and dabbling in slightly odd hobbies, he returned to feed his passion for the turf. In his notebooks he gave an account of this, and was proud to list his successes. At Maisons Lafitte and Le Tremblay racecourses, in 1922 he won almost 5,000 francs (a franc then being worth four shillings and sixpence). Still, he did insist, in his notebook, that the bookie always wins: 'I am not so devoid of common sense as to imagine that permanent financial benefit can ever be derived from backing horses.'

At times in his life as a man of the turf he experienced the lows as well as the highs, perhaps most strikingly in his horse, Lang Syne, whose fortunes typify the stressful but exhilarating life of the owner-trainer, as Harry explained in his notebook:

Joe Lowe got her apparently sound, and we took no risks but

kept her exclusively for the next year's Grand National. Four days before the race I ran down from London to Ilsley with a party of friends to see our candidate do her final gallop. … I had received, only that morning, a telegram from Roddy Owen … offering me £1,000 for Lang Syne … But this offer I refused, much to my trainer's satisfaction, until the mare, while going great guns across the downs in her final preparatory breather, suddenly blundered and fell, to rise again so hopelessly broken down that she never again appeared on a race course.

It must be remembered that £1,000 at that date would now be a value of about £40,000.

As if these pursuits were not enough to fill his life, Harry was a lecturer as well. In his recollections in *My Restless Life*, he wrote that he had given over a thousand lectures in Britain and America, and he adds:

I remember once appearing at Edinburgh on a Monday, at Glasgow on a Tuesday afternoon, and Torquay and Exeter on the afternoon and evening of the following day, at Leeds on the Thursday – Friday and Saturday at Bedford and Hull, winding up the week for the Sunday League at the Alhambra Theatre, Leicester Square, and this kind of thing was not very unusual.

He was right. He was speaking at a time when there was a positive lust for education and self-improvement. One of his fellow members of the Crimes Club, Churton Collins, led a similar life, giving fourteen lectures in one week in 1897, mainly to adult education groups.

It is not difficult to imagine Harry as a lecturer; he would have been ideal for the task, as his writing voice always brings together an entertaining brew of anecdote, factual detail and a warm, engaging human element to every assessment of what he has seen. Humour is peppered all through his travel works, with an outstanding ability to laugh at himself. One little insight into this is when he writes, in his notebooks, 'There is no doubt that works on Arctic travel would be rendered much more interesting by a detailed description of the bodily discomforts experienced by explorers in the Polar regions.' We can easily imagine a lecture given an injection of fun with that line of thought. His notebooks often give such a heightened account of minor sufferings that the result is almost surreal, as in 'Vermin and filth are now my minor miseries. Have not changed underclothes for four months.'

Chapter 10

Last Years

Seeking after that sweet golden clime,
Where the traveller's journey is done.
William Blake, *Songs of Experience*

Harry's second wife, Hilda, died at Maidenhead on 12 June 1924. Harry was then sixty-eight and retired from travelling, though he still cultivated a range of other interests, having little to do with exploration or arduous travel, and lived the life of a man about town, keeping his friendships in good repair. He was still, also, very much interested in women, and he found another wife – this time from the theatrical world.

At the Brighton Register Office on 10 November 1927, Harry married Elizabeth Ihle, a German actress. Her stage name was Elaine Inescourt, and she had appeared in small-scale productions as far back as 1898, when she was touring the provinces with a company, appearing for instance in *A Runaway Girl* at Bradford. And this was for no less than the most illustrious stage impresario of the day, George Edwardes, the Grimsby man who had made the London Gaiety Theatre into an artistic style-setting institution – far more than a mere theatre for musicals.

In 1898, Elaine had a mere mention in the reviews: the reception of the play was 'very cordial' according to one reviewer, and 'Miss Marie Fawcett plays Alice with the requisite chic. ... Amongst the other ladies, Miss Watt Tanner as Lady Coodle and Miss Elaine Inescourt are prominent.' By 1909, Elaine was still in secondary roles, but also she was involved, as so many actresses were, in productions to raise money for the suffrage cause. For instance, at the Scala Theatre, on Charlotte Street, by Tottenham Court Road, the Actresses'

Franchise League and the Women's Suffrage League combined to offer a four-hour matinee. This production included a Pageant of Famous Women, and Elaine played Hypatia, the wise daughter of the Greek philosopher, Theon.

She was a member of the Actresses' Franchise League, which had been formed in 1908, after a meeting held at the Criterion Restaurant in Piccadilly; celebrities of the stage at the time took leading roles, among them being Ellen Terry and Lena Ashwell. Their aim was to 'assist all other Leagues wherever possible'. For several years, the group joined with sister organizations such as the Women Writers' Suffrage League, and they presented plays in the least likely venues, such as in the settlements in the East End. Flora Annie Steel, a member, sums up part of the appeal of this: 'I had struck on something different from the ordinary male world, something apart from the commonplace conventional male estimate of things.' That would seem to express something fundamental in Elaine's character too.

Elaine progressed to work with several illustrious theatre companies, such as with the company led by Beerbohm Tree, for whom she played the part of Nu, the singing girl in *The Darling of the Gods*. It may well have been during the time that Harry mixed with Tree and with H.B. Irving, with whom Elaine also worked up to 1907, touring the provinces and the United States, that Harry first met Elaine, because he writes of acting as advisor to Tree when the manager was putting on a stage version of Tolstoy's novel *Resurrection*. Harry wrote that, 'Tree invited me to the Carlton restaurant to discuss local colour and to furnish him with an exact description of the dress worn by Siberian convicts.'

In 1905 Elaine did very well, taking over the role of *Leah Kleschna* from the highly rated Lena Ashwell. She had come a long way from the young woman who had started out working with the Philosophical Dramatic Society in Edinburgh. Her career was moderately successful and she performed with some of the very talented artistes of her generation.

But all this was not exactly major celebrity or even notoriety. The latter noun does apply, however, with regard to the events of late

171

August 1911, when she appeared in the divorce court. She had married John Wrightman, a dramatic critic, and he alleged misconduct on her part, referring to an affair with the writer Oliver Madox Hueffer. Elaine had married Hueffer in 1900 and they had lived in a flat on Tottenham Court Road. It appears that, on her marriage, Elaine had said she would give up her stage career, but in court in 1909, Wrightman's lawyer stated that Elaine's desire to go on the stage had been the first cause of a rift.

Back to the world of theatre she went, and in court it was explained that she had earned very well – £20 a week, in fact. In modern terms this has a value of about £1,000. Things turned sour, it seems, and then Elaine met Hueffer at a party in Paris. After a trip to Scotland, where he was born, Wrightman returned to their flat and found Elaine back home after a stay in Paris, and she confessed that in France, she and Hueffer had 'made violent love', as the lawyer put it. One press report described what happened on this revelation: 'Mr Wrightman was completely "knocked over" by the news, and on 30 December he was suffering from shock to such an extent that he had to go into a nursing home.' Apparently, Wrightman was already undergoing medical treatment for blood poisoning.

Hueffer was a very talented man: he wrote fiction under the female *nom de plume* of Jane Wardle, and as the papers reported during this court case, he had published 'some plays and written monographs on some eighteenth century painters'. He was the grandson of the great Victorian Pre-Raphaelite painter Ford Madox Brown.

The result of the hearing was an award of *decree nisi* with costs, and there was a daughter, whose custody went to Wrightman. The marriage had apparently been tortuous and from a letter quoted in the press reports, there was a complex love somewhere between the divorcees. Elaine called Wrightman 'Bunny' and wrote in one letter, 'I cannot tell you how sorry I am about the whole affair. … I wish I could undo all that has happened, but that alas is now too late.' She wanted the letter burned, but instead, there it was in print, in national newspapers in 1911.

There are plenty of pictures of Elaine, and perhaps the one with the best impression of her face is an image showing her rich dark hair and finely featured face, as she wears an elaborate stage costume hinting at an historical role.

This was the woman who was to be Harry's last wife – his companion for the last six years of his life. He retired to live in Brighton, where they had married. Elaine was forty-nine when they married. Both, it appears, had given up their professional careers, but Frieda, Elaine's daughter with Wrightman, went on to have a stage and film career, being notable for her taking the leading role in Noel Coward's *Hay Fever*.

By 1933, the couple were in Bournemouth, and Elaine's last appearance on stage before that date seems to have been in a three-act farce with Donald Wolfit at the Everyman Theatre, in 1929. We might wonder why he would choose this peaceful seaside resort on the South Coast, but the fact is that he went there to die. It is sad to think of what he could have enjoyed had he lived longer. All around him on his town strolls he could have seen images of speed, travel and modernity: there was the colourful town railway poster with its welcome – Bournemouth – the centre of health and pleasure; there was the busy Wimborne Road, where trams rattled by, and soon, there were to be trolleybuses; there was the Royal Aero Club, which used the racecourse; and perhaps most attractive of all, there was the sight of the Red Funnel boats steaming along by the pier. More everyday but still suggesting a journey was the motor coach station on Holdenhurst Road. An old picture of the place shows several boards with lists of destinations, and two men wearing long white coats and military style hats. The boarding proclaims, 'This is the chief starting point for our tours and services.' We have to wonder whether Harry saw the irony of that, now that his journeys were done, and he surely had a shiver from his memory of Siberia when he saw the poster advertising Burberry Weatherproofs, sold at the shop of Sidney Thompson on Old Christchurch Road. On that picture he would have seen a woman wrapped in a Burberry raincoat and sporting a useful hat, shielded against the elements. How he must have longed to be back in the midst of the worst weather in the world. But no, as was noted earlier, his membership of the Royal Geographical Society ended in 1925. His future was in staring at the sea, taking a stroll, and remembering those years in the wilderness.

Harry de Windt, explorer and writer, died, aged seventy-seven, in that town, on 30 November 1933, and is buried at the Cemetery Junction Graveyard. Harry and Elaine had moved to Bournemouth just nine weeks before his death, and he was taken ill in a nursing home six weeks after arrival. The *Western Morning News* simply recorded his death in a few sentences and summarized his career. The *Western Daily Press* made rather more of a feature of the event, producing an obituary headed 'Man who Went from Paris to New York By Land – Famous Explorer starts his Last Journey'. Their tribute also stressed his three marriages and his time as a camp commandant. He was a 'character' but not seen as particularly significant.

His last days were spent in the nursing home, and no doubt he was still insisting on being the raconteur, stories pouring out of him, as they always did. It would be entirely in keeping with his active life that Harry spent his last few weeks in a superior home, something akin to the classy hotels he had been used to in-between his travels. There was, for instance, the Home Sanatorium at West Southborne in the town, and this specialized in pulmonary tuberculosis. Bournemouth was a place specializing in nursing homes for TB sufferers, having three other such homes listed in a medical annual of 1923. As Harry was an 'advanced case' he was probably at the Firs Home.

We have to assume that Elaine was his nurse in the declining years. She lived on until 1964, and had done a little work over the years since Harry's death, including a radio appearance on the Home Service in 1939, *In a Gondola: A Venetian Silhouette*. She left an immense amount of money to charities, including £3,000 each to the Nurses' Fund for Nurses and the Society Promoting Welfare for the Blind. She had been known in her last years as Elaine de Windt, rather than the official 'Charlotte Elizabeth de Windt'.

Chapter 11

A Summing-Up

He spoke with a certain what-is-it in his voice, and I could
see that, if not actually disgruntled, he was far from being
gruntled.

P.G. Wodehouse, *The Code of the Woosters*

When this biography was first conceived, I was urged by a sense of having wanted to initiate a crusade – the one that surely all writers know well – the feeling that one has discovered a writer who has been unjustly neglected. I still feel that sense of injustice now, and the sense that my preceding words may at least contribute something to the status and reputation of this remarkable subject of my book, is very gratifying. Of course, so many of those forgotten writers – well read and celebrated in their times – have sunk into oblivion. Whether or not some of these writers really deserve to have their works back in print and well reviewed is a matter of opinion. But on top of any discussion regarding Harry de Windt's abilities as a writer, there is the undeniable fact that his expeditions were exceptionally bold and impressive in the late Victorian and Edwardian years.

I never felt that there was any claim to be made that Harry was exceptional in terms of his achievement when compared with other intrepid travellers and explorers: it was always a case of finding in him the qualities of the Victorian gentleman explorer. However, his birth and background in France added another interesting dimension to the enquiry into his life and thoughts. As matters turned out, it was his interior life that proved to be the dark, impenetrable journey for me; the exterior, very visible outward journey – the chronicle of his deeds – was far more accessible.

My true interest initially was in promoting knowledge of and interest in this remarkable man: here was a true individualist, a real character, and most strikingly of all perhaps, here was a writer who takes you with him on his treks, a man who shapes you into another member of his party of travellers. Imagination is still required, but he guides and directs, sure of what his story is meant to be.

Every biographer is faced with the challenge of bringing together the threads of that rich fabric that contains the individual life. In addition to that problem, there is the need to leave the reader with a sense of the completeness of the life in question, yet that is impossible, given the obvious fact that a written 'life' of any human being is merely a commentary on facts together with the string of facts themselves. In the case of Harry de Windt, there were surely more interesting facts than in the average of our 'three score years and ten' and hence his life may be summed up in a variety of ways.

Yes, looking objectively at how he spent his years, he could easily be summed up as being a selfish, self-centred man who allowed whimsical notions to become reality – in other words, that he followed his dreams. But it is hard to deny that in fact his enterprises were usually business ventures as well as manly treks across vast tracts of inhospitable terrain. This leads to a question often asked of such characters – did they feel the need of a trial, of a test of manhood? Was it simply because Harry lived in an age when science was aiming to extend knowledge of distant cultures, geography and peoples? The answer probably lies somewhere in a mix of all the possible motives.

Harry explained, each time he planned a journey, that there was a palpable everyday motive for his dangerous travel, but if we read between the lines of his other works – the writings that did not relate to the major expeditions – then there are clues about what testing, perilous journeys meant to him. One pointer to his attitudes is in his passages of contempt regarding tourism, as in *My Notebook at Home and Abroad*, where we have this:

Moreover, on a sandy space near the principal hotel, 'roundabouts', swing-boats and a shooting gallery had been provided for the wants of these unwelcome visitors; also a couple of aged and attenuated camels, bearing gaudy canopies and trappings, and tethered outside the tent of an itinerant photographer. And here, throughout the livelong day, these unfortunate animals were mounted by successive 'Arries' and 'Arriets', who, clad in appropriate desert costume … were thus able to send their suburban friends an ocular proof of the wild and perilous life they were leading!

In the course of the book, I have also raised the question as to how much military intelligence Harry may have been involved in. He admits that he did one particular task for the British Army, and refuses to specify what. What strikes one, though, is just how many influential contacts he had in his personal network of travellers and officials; if he did any undercover work, it was done with the perfect disguise – the slightly crazy Britisher journeying into the vast solitudes of the earth, where he would surely die.

His is a life with shadows, however, and that is frustrating for a biographer. The people moving around with him are thinly drawn. We have very few of their actual spoken words and only slender descriptions of them. The de Windt writings are centred on one all-consuming ego, and the reader has to relish the long journeys with him or try to resist. There is no half-measure. The traveller back in his day, of course, had to be selfish and often dictatorial, or chaos would have followed; after all, these intrepid British prisoners of wanderlust had the determination to succeed at all costs. Emotion would hinder progress.

Writing and researching this story has meant that I have had to inevitably tolerate that ego; I have had to acclimatize to his tastes, whims and predilections. He had his prejudices and preferences: who has not? But what saves him from too much predictability and familiarity is his wonderful duality of self. He insists on loving Paris and celebrating his French sensibility, while all the time he is an English gentleman, as far as the world is concerned. This does not discount the fact that he was probably not a man to cross. To organize and lead the expeditions he did, arguably there had to be steel in him as well as the surface affability he cultivated. Having said that, there is always, in his narratives, compassion, and caring in his footnotes to the main story. In the course of his Siberian travels, he had to face countless people facing death from disease and starvation, and he also had to empathize with the political exiles. This could not have been accomplished without that element of sympathetic feeling he builds into the voice of the storyteller.

How are we to rate him as a writer? The genre of travel writing has come so far in the last twenty years that he surely needs to be reassessed, and perhaps be understood as more than a mere chronicler of journeys. His prose style is workmanlike, precise and careful. He is fond of being precise and applying plenty of commas to create a style that reflects a steady deliberation, a process of thought that would suit a judge on a bench, taking time to fully comprehend what stands before him. Yet this is far from pedestrian: he is able to lift the style into lyricism when the mood takes him. One feels that his star will rise in this respect.

At the moment he is on the far boundary as a travel writer. Our current explorer-hero, Sir Ranulph Fiennes, in his book *My Heroes*, does not include even a passing mention of Harry. He has been consigned to the footnotes, and that may well be because he took his middle-ground ethos with him wherever he went, rather than complementing his narratives with a version of some radical questioning. He offered no counter-narrative than the one that he aligned himself with.

Still, appraising any writer, other than perhaps Shakespeare and Homer, is always going to be a difficult task. He was a writer at a time when no attention was paid to sorting out any kind of literary 'league table' of writers working in his genre. There is no denying that his approach to a book was to give a structured, stage-by-stage account of the chosen itinerary. Over and above that material, the narrative voice shows through as an extension of his character, and in that he was a man of his time, taking with him the bias and prejudice of his class when it came to assessing and judging other ethnic groups he met on the trail.

In the travel works, there is the absolute assumption that anecdotal experience has a valuable place in the gathering knowledge of the most obscure corners of the globe. Harry is confident that his opinions and descriptions will add to the knowledge of places, and the assurance is founded on the basic belief that knowledge is, in itself, valuable. In that he is no different from his Victorian fellow travellers.

There was always, in spite of the sheer wanderlust at the heart of Harry's reasons for travel, an ostensible motive for going somewhere, whether that was economic or commercial, or simply for the achievement, but he could never resist the urge to include material that would be usually found in guides. This is apparent most notably in his Alaskan writings, in which, on reaching the Klondike, he provides lists of essential materials and equipment.

Where he does offer some outstanding literary ability is in his assumption that the reader is his compatriot, brother Britisher, and a gentleman. Once he has assumed that in the reader, his style is easier to maintain. Of course, he had the rare advantage of being able to describe an array of material (in writers' terms) that had the value of novelty. He could constantly repeat the notion of being either the first, or at least one of the few, to see what is before his eyes. There was in his style generally an effort to recreate the allure of the spoken word found in storytelling by the fire on a cold night; but when he stretches for a lyrical, impassioned prose style, he can achieve that with real emotional power.

The one sure guide to Harry's future 'afterlife' as a writer – the rescue from oblivion most writers yearn for – is that most of his books are still in print, from the totally curious *Moles and Their Meaning*, to compendiums of his best narratives, accessible also for Kindle reading. This is not to say that he would be concerned about that, but there are intimations in his work that he did care about how his work was received. He need not have worried, as the lust for reading about distant places and other peoples goes from strength to strength. It may not be an easy task to argue that he was a ground-breaker in his genre, but he did help to establish travel writing as more than the province of the light, entertaining traveller who merely wants to give a cultural commentary – an extension of that vast literature relating to the Grand Tour that poured out of the British press in the Enlightenment and well into the nineteenth century.

There is also the nagging and lingering question of his travelling companions, who remain a most shadowy and vague group of characters, with the exception of Mackenzie, on the Balkan trip. Thanks to family history research, fragments concerning George Harding, the manservant, have emerged. For instance, at a sale run by Robert Finan in 2003, this description was in the catalogue:

> An Inuit model kayak enclosing a seated figure of an Eskimo, carved wood head with pegged body decorated in orange pigment, hide leggings – moss filled, moth damage, one glove lacking; together with a model snow shoe, and compliment of weapons, with painted wood shafts and marine ivory tips. The figure 10ins overall. … Provenance: acquired by Wm George Harding ca. 1901.

There is little more available on Harry's 'Passepartout' on the epic journey across Siberia.

As for M. De Clinchamp on that journey, he could be any one of a number of scions from that noble house in France. All we appear to have is the photo of him, standing by Harry and George, wrapped in their furs. The photographs we have of the various expeditions tend to suggest that Harry was only interested in showing the fascination with 'going to extremes' and the demands of the journey, rather than indulging in long accounts of the friendships created along the way. His books are not tales of personalities in the modern sense of travel writing, such as the 'three men in a boat' genre in which friends go together and their characters make an integral part of the journey (and the read, of course).

But the de Windt family history goes on: the Clark descendants have assembled what material they can; the Inescourt name was perpetuated in the very successful career of Elaine's daughter. Yet perhaps we may imagine Harry, in his last years in Bournemouth, dozing in an armchair and enjoying his beloved cigar and the odd gin. In those days, the caring profession was not so suffocatingly caring, and at any rate, Harry would have been too insistent to be ignored.

In the end, as I am his first biographer, I am left with very different feelings than the ones I had when I first read one of his books. Although he is still, in my mind, the absolute embodiment of the Victorian–Edwardian man of action and man of letters, he appears to have more than a shade of humour in him, as he travelled the world taking care to make the most of trains and ships when he could. Still, here was a man as much at home in a carriage full of rowdy Serbian army officers as he was among the lowliest Russian exile in a stinky *étape* several thousand miles east of Yakutsk. He was, finally, his own man; that may have cut out those who loved him rather more drastically than we might understand today, but that behaviour was yet another aspect of his time and place.

Another writer who understood the call of the wild to Alaska was the poet Robert Service, and one of his poems applies well to Harry de Windt – *The Wanderlust* – and there we find these lines:

The wanderlust has lured me to the seven lonely seas,
Had dumped me on the tailing-piles of dearth:
The wanderlust has hailed me from the morris chairs of ease,
Has hurled me to the ends of all the earth.'

There may have been ostensible motives for the de Windt expeditions – sensible, practical ones such as economic enterprises or travelling and tourist routes – but in the end, he couldn't stay in one place for long. When he did move, it was not to the next town, but to extremes. If the best travel writers 'take one with them' as an extra member of the party, then that is true of a Harry de Windt book: we take the highs and lows, just as he puts them in front of us, metaphorically sitting there, beside him.

The one remaining frustration is the marginality of the secondary players in the de Windt story – his family. It seems strongly ironical that in a massive and elaborate family tree such as that of the Brookes and de Windts, Harry's family take such a shadowy role in this biography. As with so many Victorian lives of male celebrities, the women behind them 'stood and waited' and their stories are often sketchy.

Acknowledgements

There are many people to thank here. The research required was wide-ranging and challenging; although the bulk of the events of any importance in Harry de Windt's life are recorded in his works of travel and in his notebooks, there is much else to track down.

Staff at the Brynmor Jones Library, University of Hull, were very helpful in finding some of the ephemera of the Edwardian years relating to Harry's activities; staff at Scunthorpe Library were a welcome support in searching for more obscure newspaper sources. Also, Bryan Longbone is thanked for his comments on railway history. For information regarding Harry's membership of the Royal Geographical Society, thanks go to Julie Carrington. Also, with Bartholomew's maps in mind, thanks go to the blog produced by the National Library of Scotland concerning Harry and the maps prepared for him.

Thanks are also due to the library staff at Lincolnshire Archives, regarding some of the original work relating to prisons in the Great War, and to staff at the conference centre, Swanwick, in Derbyshire, for similar sources.

Finally, as always, thanks go to my editor, Linne Matthews, who always does a very professional job in helping to streamline the storytelling.

Bibliography

Note: dates of first publication are given in brackets before the publishing details of the works cited or referred to in the text. Dates of de Windt's works given all refer to the dates of first publication.

As to the availability of Harry's works, a number of these below are now readable on Kindle; but most of his lesser-known books are still in out-of-print works and are not so easy to find. As may be seen from my listings, reading some of the travels books is quite a challenge; one would hope that reprints are being planned, but at least some companies are producing print on demand versions of some of Harry's works, as is the case with *Russia as I Know It*.

Works by Harry de Windt
A Ride to India Across Persia and Baluchistan, Chapman & Hall, London, 1891.
From Paris to New York by Land, Nelson, London, 1903.
From Pekin to Calais by Land, Chapman & Hall, London, 1889.
Moles and their Meaning (1907), Odd Books, London, 2014.
My Note-Book at Home and Abroad, Chapman & Hall, London, 1923.
My Restless Life, Grant Richards, London, 1909.
On the Equator, Cassell, Petter, Galpin & Co, London, 1882.
Russia as I Know it, Chapman & Hall, London, 1917.
Siberia as It Is, Chapman & Hall, London, 1892.
'Some Incidents of Twenty Years of Travel', *The Wide World Magazine*, London, 1902.
Through the Gold-Field of Alaska to Bering Straits, Chatto & Windus, London, 1899.
Through Savage Europe (1905), Collins, London and Glasgow, 1909.
True Tales of Travel and Adventure, Chatto & Windus, London, 1899.

BIBLIOGRAPHY

Works cited
Anon, *Your Club*, Whitbread, A.N. Holden & Co, London, 1950.
Applebaum, Anne, *Gulag: A History*, Penguin, London, 2003.
Ashcroft, Frances, *Life at the Extremes*, HarperCollins, London, 2001.
Barrows, Samuel J., *The International Prison Congress*, Government Printing Office, Washington, 1908.
Besterman, Theodore, *Crystal-Gazing*, William Rider & Son, London, 1924.
Bideleux, Robert, and Jeffries, Ian, *A History of Eastern Europe: Crisis and Change*, Routledge, Abingdon, 1998.
Butterworth, Alex, *The World that Never Was: a true story of dreamers, schemers, anarchists and secret agents*, Vintage Books, London, 2011.
Chekhov, Anton, *A Journey to Sakhalin*, Ian Faulkner Publishing, Cambridge, 1993.
Chekhov, Anton, *A Life in Letters*, Penguin, London, 2004.
Clunn, Harold P., *The Face of London*, Simpkin Marshall, London, 1932.
Cross, Anthony, *A People Passing Rude: British responses to Russian Culture*, Open Book Publishers, Cambridge, 2012.
Emmerson, Charles, *1913: The World before the Great War*, Vintage Books, London, 2013.
Fijnant, Cyrille, and Paoli, Letizia (Eds), *Organized Crime in Europe*, Springer Norwell, Massachusetts, 2004.
Green, Benny (Ed), *The Last Empires*, Pavilion, London, 1986.
Grenville, J.A.S., *A World History of the 20th Century*, HarperCollins, London, 1987.
Izzard, Molly, *Freya Stark*, Sceptre, London, 1993.
Keay, John, *Eccentric Travellers*, John Murray, London, 1982.
Kennan, George, *Siberia and the Exile System*, The Century Co, New York, 1891.
Koss, Stephen, *The Rise and Fall of the Press in Britain*, University of North Carolina Press, 1981.
MacQueen-Pope, W., *Ghosts and Greasepaint*, Robert Hale, London, 1951.

185

Meignan, Victor, *De Paris a Pékin par Terre: Siberie-Mongolie*, E. Plon at Cie, Paris, 1876.

Murray, Nicholas, *A Corkscrew is Most Useful*, Little, Brown, London, 2008.

Patrick, Chris, and Baister, Stephen, *William Le Queux: Master of Mystery*, the authors, no date.

Pemberton, Max, *Sixty Years ago and After*, Hutchinson, London, 1936.

Pfeiffer, Ida, *A Lady's Voyage Around the World*, Ebury Press, London, 1988.

Powter, Geoff, *We Cannot Fail*, Robinson, London, 2006.

Randall, C.C., *The International Prison Congress: St. Petersburg, Russia*, General Printing Office, Washington, 1891.

Rice, Edward, *Captain Sir Richard Francis Burton*, Da Capo Press, Cambridge, MA, 2001.

Service, Robert, *Collected Verse of Robert Service* (1930), Ernest Benn, London, 1953.

Thubron, Colin, *In Siberia*, Penguin Books, London, 2000.

Thubron, Colin, *The Lost Heart of Asia*, Penguin, London, 1994.

Turgeney, Ivan, *Three Novellas*, Farrar, Straus & Giroux, New York, 1968.

Wellesley, Frederick, *Recollections of a Soldier-Diplomat*, Hutchinson, London, 1932.

General Works

Baedeker, Carl, *Austria-Hungary*, Baedeker, Leipzig, 1905.

Bott, Alan, *Our Fathers 1870–1900*, Heinemann, London, 1901.

Cockcroft, Irene, and Croft, Susan, *Art, Theatre and Women's Suffrage*, Aurora Metro Press, Twickenham, 2010.

Dobson, Mary, *Murderous Contagion: a human history of disease*, Quercus, London, 2015.

Daunton, Mark, *The Organisation of Knowledge in Victorian Britain*, Oxford University Press, 2005.

Dostoievski, Fyodor, *Memoirs from the House of the Dead* (1861–62), Oxford University Press, 1965.

Freeman, William, *The Life of Lord Alfred Douglas: spoilt child of genius*, Herbert Joseph Ltd, London, 1948.

Griffiths, Arthur, *Secrets of the Prison-House*, Chapman & Hall, London, 1894.

Herber, Mark, *Legal London: A Pictorial History*, Phillimore, London, 1999.

Hopkirk, Peter, *The Great Game*, Oxford University Press, 1991.

Hughes, William, *The Advanced Class-Book of Modern Geography*, George Philip, London, 1908.

Hulme, Peter, and Youngs, Tim, *The Cambridge Companion to Travel Writing*, Cambridge University Press, 2002.

James, Lawrence, *The Rise and Fall of the British Empire*, Abacus, London, 1995.

London Maps: Medieval to Twentieth Century, Old House Books, London, 2010.

Lynch, Michael, *Reaction and Revolution: Russia 1881–1924*, Hodder & Stoughton, Abingdon, 2000.

Medical Annual, The, The Medical Annual, Bristol, 1923.

Mee, Arthur, *Harmsworth History of the World*, Harmsworth, London, 1907.

Mullen, Richard, and Munson, James, *The Smell of the Continent*, Pan Macmillan, London, 2010.

Oliver, James A., *The Bering Strait Crossing: A 21st Century Frontier between East and West*, Information Architects, London, 2006.

Stobart, Mrs St Clair, *War and Women*, G.Bell & Sons Ltd, London, 1913.

Winder, Robert, *Bloody Foreigners: the story of immigration in Britain*, Little, Brown, London, 2004.

Journal Sources

Hudson, Roger, 'In Focus: The New York to Paris Race 1908', *History Today*, April 2014, pp. 22–3.

Morris, A.J.A., 'Spender, John Alfred', *Oxford Dictionary of National Biography* (online), 2004–15.

Stead, W.T., 'Madame Olga Novikoff', *The Review of Reviews*, Vol. III, February 1891, pp. 123–36.

Stults, Taylor, 'George Kennan: Russian Specialist of the 1890s', *Russian Review*, Vol. 29, No. 3, July 1970, pp. 275–85.

Newspaper Sources

'Explorer Dead', *Western Morning News and Daily Gazette*, 2 December 1933, p. 7.

'Man who went from Paris to New York by Land', *Western Daily Press and Bristol Mirror*, 2 December 1933, p. 4.

Manuscript Sources

Hayes Conference Centre: 'Our History' company publication, Hayes, Swanwick, Derbyshire, 2015.

Letter from De Windt to Richard Caton Woodville, 12 December 1900, author's collection.

Mss Letters of Harry de Windt to Lord Alfred Douglas, Magdalen College: MC:P204/1/4C/2.

Internet Sources

www.britishhistoryonline.org

https://oddbooks.co.uk

www.morbidanatomymuseum.org/

Crescente, Joe, 'The Great Eastern Journey of Tsar Nicholas II in Russia Beyond the Headlines', www.rbth.co.uk

The Times Digital Archive, 'The International Prison Congress', 4 July 1872, p. 5, issue 27420 Col. E., http://infotrac.galegroup.com/itw/infomark

Index